Spain

Spain

By Barbara A. Somervill

Enchantment of the World™
Second Series

Children's Press®

An Imprint of Scholastic Inc.

New York Toronto London Auckland Sydney
Mexico City New Delhi Hong Kong
Danbury, Connecticut

Frontispiece: Casa Batlló, designed by Antoni Gaudí, Barcelona

Consultant: Luis Martín-Estudillo, Associate Professor and Director of Graduate Studies, Associate Editor, Hispanic Issues, Department of Spanish and Portuguese, The University of Iowa, Iowa City, Iowa

Please note: All statistics are as up-to-date as possible at the time of publication.

Book production by The Design Lab

Library of Congress Cataloging-in-Publication Data
Somervill, Barbara A.
  Spain/by Barbara A. Somervill.
      p. cm.—(Enchantment of the world, second series)
  Includes bibliographical references and index.
  ISBN 978-0-531-27546-7 (library binding)
  1. Spain—Juvenile literature. I. Title.
  DP17.S56 2013
  946—dc23   2012000514

1 2 3 4 5 6 7 8 9 10 R 22 21 20 19 18 17 16 15 14 13

Spain

Contents

Cover photo:
Bullfight

Pyrenees

Lammergeier

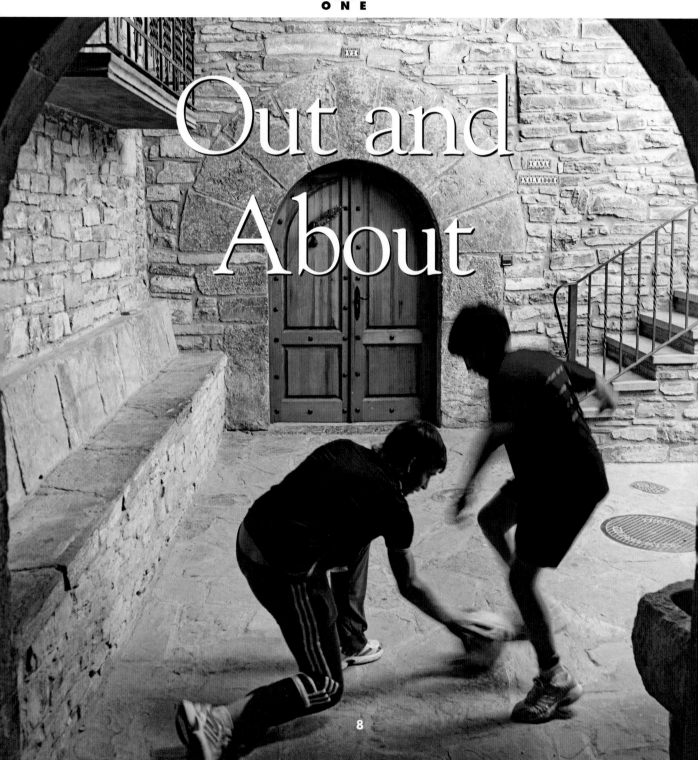

Out and About

8

PALOMA AND ISABELA PULL THEIR METRO PASSES FROM their jeans pockets and hop on the train. It is late Sunday morning, and the girls are headed to El Rastro, Madrid's gigantic flea market. El Rastro sells everything from cheap T-shirts to knockoff designer handbags to valuable antiques.

The teens will spend several hours browsing among the hundreds of stalls of El Rastro. It is likely they will see some of their friends there and, when the market closes at 3:00 p.m., go off in a group to one of the many tapas restaurants in La Latina section of Madrid.

The port of Vigo, in northwestern Spain, is one of the largest fishing ports in Europe. Vigo is home port to three fishing vessels owned by the Sánchez family. While tourists sleep, Jaime and his father rise at 2:30 a.m. They have a quick breakfast of bread, cheese, and fruit. They hurry down to their boat and head out for a long day at sea.

During the summer, Jaime fishes with his father every day. At twelve years old, he already knows how to steer a course,

Opposite: **Boys play soccer in the town of El Pueyo de Araguás in the Pyrenees.**

Tapas

Tapas are Spanish finger foods, tasty snacks that can be just about anything from a roasted potato to a skewer of chicken or a grilled onion. Tapas may be hot or cold. People usually order several tapas dishes. The tapas offered vary from region to region. Stuffed mussels, squid, and shrimp are popular along the coasts, while chorizo (sausage) is always available inland. In Basque country, tapas are also called *pinchos*.

read the GPS that shows where schools of fish are found, and mend the nets used to haul in monkfish, tuna, and mackerel. It is hard work, but Jaime is preparing for his future. He expects to be captaining his own fishing vessel by the time he is twenty. Fishing is in his blood.

Rafa and Xavi have had a stroke of luck. Xavi's uncle had tickets to see the soccer team Real Madrid play Barcelona on their home field, and he couldn't use them. So, he gave them to Xavi and his friend. At age fourteen, the boys are in their second two-year cycle at secondary school, the Spanish equivalent of high school. They study math, science, language, and history, but their real joy is playing soccer on the school team. Going to see their heroes play is a treat.

Barcelona is one of Europe's most successful clubs. Tickets to Fútbol Club Barcelona games are expensive. The closer the seats are to the field, the more expensive the tickets are. The seats Rafa and Xavi have cost € 207 ($277) each.

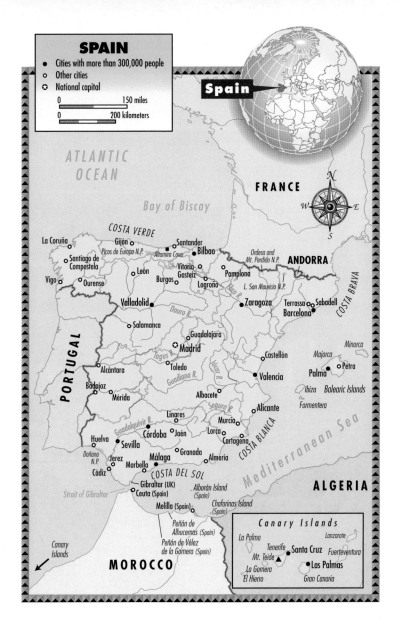

SPAIN

- Cities with more than 300,000 people
- Other cities
- National capital

0   150 miles
0   200 kilometers

Spain

ATLANTIC OCEAN

FRANCE

Bay of Biscay

COSTA VERDE

La Coruña
Gijón
Santander
Picos de Europa N.P.
Altamira Cave
Bilbao
Santiago de Compostela
Vitoria-Gasteiz
Pamplona
León
Burgos
Logroño
Vigo
Ourense
Ordesa and Mt. Perdido N.P.
ANDORRA
L. San Mauricio N.P.
Valladolid
Douro R.
Zaragoza
Terrassa Sabadell
Barcelona
COSTA BRAVA
Salamanca
Guadalajara
Madrid
Tagus R.
Toledo
Alcántara
Castellón
Majorca
Minorca
Petra
Palma
Valencia
Badajoz
Mérida
Guadiana R.
Albacete
Ibiza
Balearic Islands
Formentera
Segura R.
Alicante
Linares
Murcia
COSTA BLANCA
Guadalquivir R.
Córdoba
Jaén
Lorca
Cartagena
Huelva
Sevilla
Doñana N.P.
Jerez
Granada
Almería
Málaga
Marbella
Cádiz
COSTA DEL SOL
Gibraltar (UK)
Ceuta (Spain)
Strait of Gibraltar
Alborán Island (Spain)
Mediterranean Sea
ALGERIA
Melilla (Spain)
Chafarinas Island (Spain)
Peñón de Alhucemas (Spain)
Peñón de Vélez de la Gomera (Spain)
Canary Islands
MOROCCO

PORTUGAL

Canary Islands
La Palma
Tenerife
Lanzarote
Santa Cruz
Fuerteventura
Mt. Teide
La Gomera
El Hierro
Las Palmas
Gran Canaria

Spanish teens are more independent than most teens in the United States or Canada. Many teens spend their free hours *en la calle*—on the street. They hang out with friends, go shopping, eat, dance, and listen to music. They're out and about, ready to take advantage of everything their vibrant country has to offer.

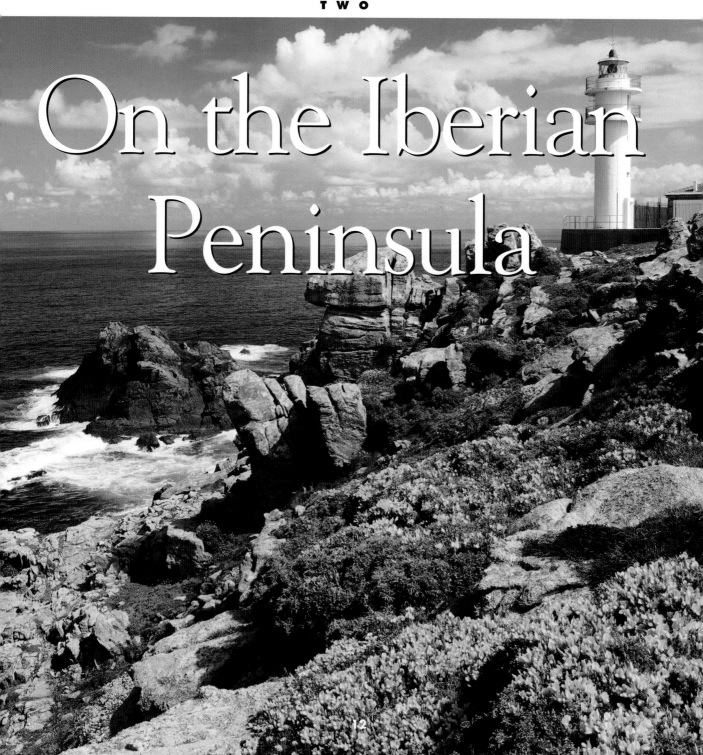

On the Iberian Peninsula

I N SOUTHEASTERN SPAIN, THE SUN HEATS WHITE sand beaches, while the gentle Mediterranean Sea laps the shore. In Spain's northwest corner, sheer cliffs drop down into an angry Atlantic Ocean. Between those two extremes lie mountain ranges, about 1,800 rivers and streams, and a high plateau.

Spain occupies nearly 85 percent of the Iberian Peninsula, a block of land that juts out from the southwestern edge of Europe. At Spain's northern border are France, Andorra, and the Atlantic Ocean. Curving around to the west are more stretches of Atlantic Ocean coastline and Portugal. To the south and east lies the Mediterranean Sea.

The bulk of Spain is on the mainland, but Spain also includes the Balearic and Canary Islands, and several small sections in northern Africa: Ceuta, the Chafarinas Islands, Melilla, Peñón de Vélez, and Alhucemas. The Balearic Islands form an archipelago—an island chain—in the Mediterranean just east of Spain. The four largest islands are Majorca, Minorca, Ibiza, and Formentera. The Canary Islands, also an archipelago, are

Opposite: **Part of the coast in northwestern Spain is called Costa da Morte, "Coast of Death," because many ships have wrecked along its dangerous, rocky shore.**

Ceuta and Melilla

Ceuta and Melilla (right) are tiny settlements in North Africa that came under Spanish rule as Spain stretched its power southward. Melilla was conquered in 1497 and Ceuta in 1668. At one point, Spain also ruled the North African city-states of Oran, Algiers, Bugia, Tripoli, and Tunis. Over the centuries, the nation lost most of its African holdings, but it has kept Ceuta and Melilla, despite Morocco's attempts to gain them back.

an arc of volcanic islands lying to the west of North Africa. Spain's tallest mountain, the volcano Mount Teide, soars 12,198 feet (3,718 meters) above the island of Tenerife, the largest and most populated of the seven Canary Islands.

Spain stretches across about 194,897 square miles (504,781 square kilometers) of land. Because it sits on a peninsula, Spain has a long coastline. Along the Mediterranean are 1,038 miles (1,670 km) of sandy beaches. In the northwest, 1,388 miles (2,234 km) of coastline feature ragged cliffs, deep-water ports, and fierce winds. Massive storms form in the Atlantic Ocean and batter the Bay of Biscay on the northern coast throughout the winter.

Regions of Spain

Spain is divided into four distinct regions: the north, the east, the south, and the Meseta Central (the inner plateau). Each region has a distinct appearance and climate. The people who live in each region have distinct customs and foods.

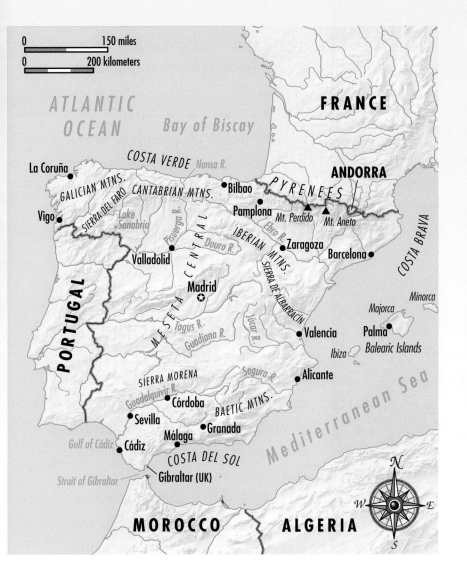

The north stretches from the Pyrenees in the east to the Atlantic Ocean in the west. The land covers about one-tenth of Spain's mainland. Its few large cities are found along the coast. Only 17 percent of Spain's population lives in the

Spaniards and visitors alike crowd Mediterranean beaches.

north. The climate is mild but very wet, as Atlantic storms bring heavy rainfall.

The east runs along the Mediterranean Sea and is heavily populated. While the region covers only 15 percent of Spain's land, it has nearly 30 percent of its population. Barcelona, Valencia, and Alicante are among the cities of the eastern region. The climate tends to be mild and fairly dry.

The south contains the lands of Andalusia. The Sierra Morena, an east-to-west mountain range at the base of the Meseta Central, separates the southern region from the rest of Spain. This region is extremely dry and suffers long periods of drought. At the southernmost point of the region, the Strait of Gibraltar offers entry into the Mediterranean Sea. This southern tip of Spain lies only 8 miles (13 km) from Africa.

Much of the central region, the Meseta, is farmland. It is the least populated region of Europe. Surrounded by mountain ranges, this region has two major seasons: a long winter and a hot summer. The Meseta occupies most of the land in Spain, yet less than 30 percent of the population lives there. The majority of the people live in Madrid or in that city's suburbs.

Mountains, Rivers, and Lakes

Spain is covered with mountain ranges, high plateaus, and steep cliffs. Nearly one-quarter of the country is at least 3,000 feet (1,000 m) above sea level.

Farm fields stretch across the Meseta in central Spain.

Even though the Pyrenees are not among the highest mountains in the world, they are nearly impassable. The rugged peaks have only a few valleys that allow passage between them. The tallest include Aneto Peak, at 11,168 feet (3,404 m), and Mount Perdido, at 11,008 feet (3,355 m). When the snow melts on the peaks each spring, waterfalls cascade down the mountainsides, filling rivers that rush toward the sea.

The Pyrenees form a natural boundary between Spain and France.

Almost directly west of the Pyrenees lie the Cantabrian Mountains, an arc of peaks that run to the Bay of Biscay, where there are shear drops as great as 3,000 feet (900 m) down to the coast. The Cantabrians form the northern border of the Meseta plateau region. From the eastern edge of the Cantabrians, another mountain system called the Iberian Cordillera heads southward. It extends nearly to the shore of the Mediterranean. The cordillera is craggy, rough, and fairly barren. Two more mountain systems, the Sierra Morena and Baetic Cordillera, lie to the south and east of the Meseta and run into the southern end of the Iberian Cordillera.

Rivers and Lakes

About 1,800 rivers and streams cut through Spain's mountain ranges, carving valleys on their way to the sea. Many of these rivers are tributaries of Spain's five major river systems: the Ebro, Douro, Tagus, Guadiana, and Guadalquivir. Of these rivers, only the Ebro empties into the Mediterranean Sea. The others drain into the Atlantic Ocean.

The Cave of Altamira

A cave in the cliffs of the Cantabrian Mountains high above the Bay of Biscay provided shelter for prehistoric humans beginning about thirty-seven thousand years ago. The Altamira cave consists of 886 feet (270 m) of rooms connected by winding passages. The walls are decorated with hunting scenes drawn by early cave dwellers and feature bison, boars, and deer. About twelve thousand years ago, a landslide blocked the cave's entrance, preserving the cave art. Altamira was discovered in 1868 by a hunter, but the paintings weren't found until 1879. It was the first cave discovered with such extensive artwork.

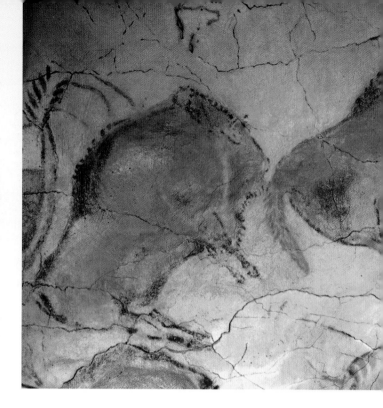

The longest river completely in Spain is the Ebro, which runs 565 miles (910 km) from the Cantabrian Mountains to the Mediterranean Sea. The Ebro begins at the Pico de Tres Mares (Peak of Three Seas), a lake that feeds three rivers: the Ebro, Pisuerga, and Nansa.

On the Iberian Peninsula, the Tagus rises only about 90 miles (145 km) from the Mediterranean shore in the Iberian Cordillera and then flows westward through Portugal to the ocean. It is the longest river on the peninsula, measuring 630 miles (1,014 km), although only 445 miles (716 km) flow through Spain. Twenty-nine miles (47 km) of the Tagus form part of the border between Spain and Portugal. In Spain, the Tagus passes through Toledo and Alcántara and flows near Madrid.

The Guadalquivir River gets its name from the Arabic Wadi al-Kabir, meaning "great river." The Guadalquivir is distinguished by abundant plant and animal life, which thrives in the river basin, and its nearly eight hundred tributaries. Near the coast, the river basin, is riddled with swampy wetlands, which are home to deer and thousands of wading birds and waterfowl.

Spain has 444 mountain lakes and 82 karst lakes. Karst lakes are mountain lakes that have no streams flowing in or out of them. They are seasonal lakes, usually fed by melting snow or glacier ice. Spain's largest lake is the Sanabria, one of the very few natural lakes in the country. It covers 909 acres (368 hectares) and was formed by glacial meltwater. Sanabria lies in the Sierra de la Culebra mountain range in the Zamora province. Most of the lakes in Spain were formed when rivers were dammed up.

Sanabria Lake is protected as part of Sanabria Lake Natural Park. The lake is home to many kinds of fish, including trout, barbel, and bream.

Spain's Volcanic Islands

Millions of years ago, volcanic eruptions in the Atlantic Ocean spewed enough lava to build the Canary Islands, a string of islands 60 miles (100 km) west of the African coastline. There is still occasionally volcanic activity near or on the islands of Tenerife, Lanzarote, El Hierro, and La Palma. An underwater eruption off the coast of El Hierro in November 2011 was accompanied by hundreds of small earthquakes. Other volcanoes in the Canary Islands have been dormant for centuries and are slowly eroding.

Hot and Cold, Wet and Dry

Winter or summer, the most pleasant climate in Spain is usually along the Mediterranean Sea. Winters are mild with daytime temperatures around 60 degrees Fahrenheit (16 degrees Celsius) and nighttime temperatures close to freezing. Summers see high temperatures of 80°F to 85°F (27°C to 30°C). Rainfall along the coast is moderate, with most rain falling in the spring and fall. Occasionally it snows along the coast of Catalonia in the northeast. In 2010, Barcelona was hit with its heaviest snowfall in twenty-five years—20 inches (50 centimeters)—which closed roads and schools.

Along the northern and western coastlines, summer temperatures are similar to those along the Mediterranean. Winters are also mild, with temperatures rarely dipping below freezing. Rainfall, however, is much greater. Asturias, for example, gets an average of 5 inches (13 cm) in October, more than twice as much as Valencia.

A Look at Spain's Cities

Barcelona is Spain's second-largest city, with a population of 1,673,075. It is the capital of the Catalonia region in northeastern Spain and a cultural and economic center of Spain. Barcelona is one of the most visited cities in Europe. People flock there to visit the old city, called the Gothic Quarter, which has many buildings dating back to medieval times. The city is also noted for its unique modern architecture, particularly works designed by Antoni Gaudí. His Sagrada Familia church (right) features curving, almost lifelike forms.

Valencia, Spain's third-largest city, has a population of 809,267. Valencia began as a Roman colony in 138 BCE. The city is a mix of medieval buildings and modern architecture. Sitting on the Mediterranean

coast, it is a major port and a tourist destination. The city is known for its Carnival-like Las Fallas festival and its traditional dish, paella, a mix of seafood and rice.

Sevilla (left) has a population of 705,107, making it the nation's fourth-largest city. Sevilla is the capital of Andalusia, in southern Spain. Moors, who were Muslims from North Africa, gained control of Sevilla in 712 CE and remained until 1248, when they were forced out. Many magnificent examples of Moorish architecture remain there. One of the prides of Sevilla is the Alcázar, a palace that was built to be a Moorish fort.

Inland, the weather is not as mild. Snow falls heavily in the mountains during the winter months. Summers see temperatures soaring to nearly 100°F (38°C). The northern Meseta has two rainy seasons: April to June and October to November. During the summer, the Meseta gets less than 0.5 inches (1.27 cm) of rain.

Conservation

Water and air pollution and habitat loss have caused significant decreases in plant and animal populations across Spain. In addition, many animal species suffer from poisoning—sometimes accidental and sometimes not. Hunting is a popular sport in Spain, and some people own private game preserves. They put out poisoned bait to reduce the number of foxes and wolves

Red foxes live throughout most of Europe and much of Asia and North America.

that prey on the animals they want to hunt. But other species also consume the bait and die. In addition, animals that feed on the bodies of the poisoned foxes and wolves are also poisoned. In recent years, the Ministry of the Environment has recorded more than one thousand animal deaths from illegal poisoning, and four in ten of those animals were protected species. Among the endangered species affected have been large birds such as red kites, imperial eagles, and lammergeiers.

Since the 1990s, Spain has been focused on conserving its natural resources. Tourism in national parks and preserves has proven to be both a blessing and a curse. Increased interest in the environment draws Europeans to national preserves, but the sheer numbers of visitors make maintaining the sites' natural states difficult. More than 650,000 people visit Ordesa National Park in the Pyrenees each year. The Doñana wetlands, on the southwestern coast, draws about 400,000 visitors per year. Both parks are home to many endangered species, such as the Iberian lynx, and human traffic puts conservation efforts at risk.

Flamingos feed in the Doñana wetlands. These wetlands are an important refuge for many endangered species, including Iberian lynxes and imperial eagles.

Magnificent Life

Two golden eyes peek through the reeds of Doñana's wetlands. The eyes disappear, as the reeds shake gently in the breeze. Moments later, a furry, rusty orange figure pounces. An Iberian lynx grasps a rabbit in its jaws. Tonight, the cat will eat well.

The Iberian lynx is the most critically endangered cat in the world. Only about three hundred are left. The lynx once thrived from the Pyrenees to the Mediterranean. Over the centuries, humans hunted the lynx for its fur, and its population declined. Part of the problem in preserving the lynx is that it is a picky eater. It eats only rabbits, and thirty other predators in lynx territories also feed on rabbits. In recent years, the rabbit population has declined by nearly 90 percent due to two major diseases and overhunting. As the rabbit population declined, so did the population of the Iberian lynx.

The Iberian lynx is one of the rarest creatures in Spain. But hundreds of other species thrive in the nation's grasslands, mountains, wetlands, and waters.

Opposite: **A male lynx needs to eat one rabbit a day. A female with cubs likely needs three rabbits.**

The National Flower

In Spain, blood-red carnations send a message: My heart aches for you. The red carnation is the national flower of Spain. It symbolizes love, hope, and faithfulness. Flamenco dancers often wear carnations while they perform their passionate dances.

Grasslands

Savannas and grasslands cover about 22 percent of Spain, mostly in plains or river valleys. The largest grassland region lies along the Guadalquivir. This is also the best farmland in Spain, and most of the natural grasses have been plowed under to make way for cities and farms. Grasslands are also found in the La Mancha Plain along the Guadiana and in the high meadows of the Sierra Nevada.

Rabbits, rodents, and ground birds thrive in shrublands and deep grasses. Partridges and red grouse nest in dense grass, their feathers providing them with camouflage. Even so, wily red foxes still find the nests and steal the eggs. Iberian lynxes hunt rabbits, competing with Iberian eagles, royal owls, and Montagu's harriers in order to get a good meal.

Along the eastern coast, the matorral—a dense, shrub-covered landscape—is a mix of native herbs, low-lying trees, and tufts of grasslike plants. Tree heather grows side by side with rose garlic, common thyme, and Jerusalem sage. Yellow bee orchids and mirror orchids sprinkle yellow and purple across the land. Brushy Spanish broom bends under the weight of thousands of small yellow flowers in the spring and summer.

The matorral displays a full cycle of natural life. It attracts honeybees and a variety of other insects. Butterflies, like the swallowtail, flit from flower to flower. Dartford warblers and bee-eaters gobble up insects while mice and rats find plenty of food in the seedpods of the thick shrubs. In turn, ladder snakes feed on the rodents that live in the matorral. Human visitors need to be careful in this landscape—scorpions hide under rocks and fallen limbs from holm oak trees.

Spanish lavender is one of many kinds of flowers that brighten the land in the matorral.

Spain's mountains support a variety of life. Pines flourish in some mountain ranges, while beeches, chestnut trees, and oaks dominate other forests in the Pyrenees and the Cantabrians.

Beech forests are home to a wide range of small mammals, songbirds, and birds of prey. Eagle owls and beech martens are nighttime predators in the mountain regions. Golden orioles hide in the leaf cover of old growth beech forests.

Chestnut trees are tall, with fewer branches and leaves than beeches or oaks, and produce plenty of tasty nuts. In a year with ample rainfall, oaks yield millions of acorns that drop to the forest floor below. More than three hundred animal species feed on acorns, including wild boars, red squirrels, and nuthatches. Wild boars also feast on chestnuts, as do dormice and field mice.

Above the tree line, mountain cliffs attract chamois, a wild goat that lives in small groups and feeds on grass and flowers.

The Imperial Eagle

The Spanish imperial eagle, also known as Adalbert's eagle, is a highly threatened species that lives mainly in central and southwest Spain. The eagles prey on rabbits, partridges, rodents, crows, and ducks. Imperial eagles do not migrate, so a decline in local prey populations seriously affects the species. Currently, about three hundred pairs of imperial eagles remain in Spain. The species faces threats from loss of habitat, reduced prey populations, illegal poisoning, and collisions with utility poles.

They share their rocky homes with lammergeiers, eagle owls, and griffon vultures. Lammergeiers and griffon vultures feed on the carcasses (dead bodies) of other animals. They are two of the largest birds among Spain's bird species.

Chamois live on rocky mountainsides. They are well suited to this environment and can run 30 miles per hour (50 kph) over the steep, uneven land.

Wetlands

Spain's many rivers flow into the Atlantic Ocean or the Mediterranean Sea. At the mouths of these rivers, salt marshes and freshwater wetlands form. Wetlands are land covered with several inches of water. These ecosystems serve as a natural filter, cleaning pollution from rivers. They also serve as a nursery for fish and crustaceans.

Quebrantahuesos

The Spanish name for lammergeiers is *quebrantahuesos*, or bone breakers. They are the largest birds of prey in Europe and the rarest species of the vulture family. About 70 percent of Spain's lammergeier population—only eighty breeding pairs—lives in the Spanish Pyrenees. To lure lammergeiers to move into other Spanish mountains, conservationists built nests that the birds could take over. They also made life-size models of the birds and installed them on cliffs. These tactics appear to have worked. Once on the brink of extinction, lammergeier populations have begun to rebound. The birds have been seen in northern mountain regions, including the Cantabrian Mountains.

Nearly all the salt marsh wetlands in Europe are located in Spain. Centuries ago, wetlands covered about 1 percent of Spain's land. Most of the original wetlands have been drained for agriculture or human needs. Spain's 150,000 wetlands are small, each covering only a few acres of land. Wetlands are nesting sites for many species of waterfowl, including ducks, geese, and shelducks. They are also winter homes for many species of migrating wading birds, such as purple herons, cranes, spoonbills, and egrets, all of which nest in northern Europe during summer months. Flamingos use Spanish wetlands as rest stops to get away from the intensely hot summers in Africa. These birds feed on the fish and crustaceans that breed in salt marshes.

Spain's most diverse wetland is the nature preserve at Doñana. This site on the southern coast has three kinds of

Cork Oaks

The corks used to seal wine bottles are actually the spongy bark of the cork oak tree. Cork oaks are green year-round and grow up to 65 feet (20 m) tall. The trees have two layers of bark. The inside layer allows water and sap to flow through the tree trunk. The outside layer is the spongy, light brown substance that is used for corkboards and bottle stoppers.

ecosystems: swamps, scrublands, and shifting sand dunes on beaches. It has such diverse life that it is unique in Europe. The largest populations of Iberian lynx and Spanish imperial eagles live in Doñana. Fallow deer, red deer, wild boars, badgers, and mongooses also make their homes there.

Spoonbills are one of the many bird species that feed at the Doñana wetlands. They use their flat bills to snatch insects, fish, and other creatures from the water.

The waters near the Balearic Islands are rich with sea life.

Coastal Waters

Because Spain has two long coastlines and two island groups, the country has plentiful marine life. Atlantic waters still support schools of Spanish mackerel and bluefin tuna. Commercial fishers travel farther from shore to harvest clams, mussels, and oysters, as well as red mullet, elvers, and octopuses. Whales and dolphins are common in the Atlantic coastal waters.

Scuba divers off Spain's mainland coast and the Balearic Islands can expect to see crabs, lobsters, and shrimp scuttling along the seafloor. Octopuses, eels, and squid hide in reefs. Huge groupers swim in the clear waters, along with cardinal fish, damselfish, and rainbow wrasses. Mediterranean sea life struggles against the expanding threat of caulerpa, an invasive seaweed that has no natural predators in the sea. Caulerpa has become a true monster of the deep. It chokes all other seaweed and is toxic to many native fish and seafood species.

The waters around the Canary Islands teem with life. Lime urchins scuttle across the seafloor, while bottlenose dolphins leap and dive along the islands' coastlines. One of the most thrilling sights of the Canaries is the number of sea turtles that swim in local waters. Loggerheads, green sea turtles, hawksbills, leatherbacks, and Kemp's ridleys frequent the waters.

Common dolphins near the Canary Islands. Dolphins typically live in large groups, called pods.

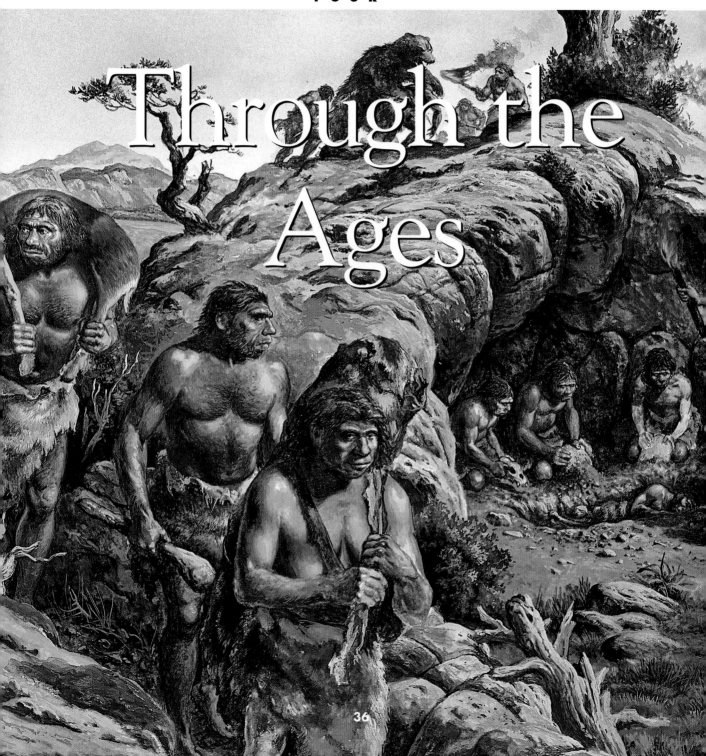

Through the Ages

I N 2007 AND 2008, ARCHAEOLOGISTS DISCOVERED a tooth and a jawbone that pushed Spain's history back a million years. These human remnants, which are 1.2 million years old, were found in Atapuerca, in the northern part of the country. Another bone found nearby dates back 1.3 million years. These remains are some of the oldest hominid (humanlike) bones ever found. Before these discoveries, it was believed that hominids were in Europe no earlier than about half a million years ago.

Opposite: **Neanderthals died out between twenty-four and twenty-eight thousand years ago.**

Prehistoric Populations

From 706,000 to 22,000 years ago, early human groups of Neanderthals thrived in the natural caves of Spain's mountain ranges. These people were hunter-gatherers who moved in search of large game. They used stone tools to make spearheads and cutting tools. Thin bones were made into fishhooks. Neanderthals could make fire and most likely cooked their meat. Those who lived along the coast ate fish and hunted seals and dolphins. Those who lived inland hunted wild boar, deer, and bison.

Cro-Magnon humans replaced the Neanderthals. For more than twenty thousand years, they lived in the caves of Altamira in northern Spain. They spent time deep in the caves painting the walls with yellow ochre, charcoal, and rust-red hematite. They illustrated one of the most important events in their lives: hunting. Pictures show horses, bison, goats, and other animals along with handprints of the artists.

Cro-Magnon people hunted using harpoons or spears. They developed basic bows and arrows. They also developed musical instruments, including bone flutes, drums, and bullroarers, which consist of a stick or stone attached to leather string. A bullroarer makes a roaring or humming sound when it is swung in the air.

Cro-Magnon people painted the shape of their hands on the walls of caves in Europe. This modern-day model shows how the painting was done.

Traders, Invaders, Raiders

By 1000 BCE, people living on the Iberian Peninsula had built towns along the coast. Although people continued to hunt and fish, they also raised farm animals and planted crops. In addition, they traded with people from other parts of the Mediterranean. The Phoenicians were a seagoing people from what is now Lebanon, a nation in the eastern Mediterranean. They brought ivory, oils, and perfumes, which they traded for Iberian goods made of bronze and silver.

As Iberian goods became known throughout the Mediterranean, more traders came to Spain, bringing new products to the Iberian Peninsula. The Greeks brought olive oil, pottery, and enslaved workers to trade. The people of Carthage, a powerful civilization in North Africa, brought purple dye, amber, tin, and silver to trade. As trade increased, Spain became richer and of greater interest to the primary invaders of the era, the Romans.

In 218 BCE, Rome swarmed the Iberian Peninsula from the south. Spain fell under Roman control for seven hundred years. The Romans brought their knowledge of architecture to the Iberian Peninsula. They built roads and bridges that connected the towns of their domain, and aqueducts that carried water from rivers to cities. The Romans also brought their language, which is the basis of modern Spanish.

Romans began to lose control of their empire in western Europe in the 400s, when Germanic tribes began moving to new areas. In 573 CE, a group called the Visigoths invaded Roman Spain. They were the first invaders to attack the Iberian Peninsula by coming through the Pyrenees.

The Visigoths were Christians. They built many churches, some of which still survive. San Pedro de la Nave, near Campillo, is almost completely intact.

The Visigoths were also accomplished jewelers. They made beautifully carved pins, large gold crowns, and jeweled belts. The Spanish continued to be known for these skills long after the Visigoths lost control of the region.

The Aqueduct in Segovia

Most of what Rome built in Spain has disappeared over time, but the aqueduct in Segovia still stands as a reminder of the greatness of Roman architecture. Built in the second century BCE, the aqueduct measures about 3,000 feet (900 m) long. The shape and placement of the stones holds the aqueduct together. There is no mortar or any other material holding the stones in place.

The Moors Arrive

At the end of the seventh century CE, Arab armies were advancing across North Africa. In Spain, these people became known as Moors. In 711, the Moorish armies crossed the Strait of Gibraltar to the Iberian Peninsula. Led by Tariq ibn Ziyad, they marched across the land, forcing the Visigoths from power. By 714, most of the Iberian Peninsula was under the Moors' control.

Unlike the Visigoths, the Moors were Muslim, followers of the religion Islam. Muslim Spain was called Al-Andalus. Many native Spaniards converted to Islam. It is likely that by the year 1000 the majority of people in Al-Andalus were Muslim.

The Visigoth church San Pedro de la Nave dates back to the seventh century.

Important cities in Al-Andalus, such as Córdoba, Granada, and Sevilla, were among the leading European cities of the time. They were centers of culture and learning. People of various cultural backgrounds made great contributions. Scholars in Al-Andalus helped revive classical Greek learning. Poetry, philosophy, and science thrived. In the eleventh century, prominent astronomer Abu Ishaq Ibrahim ibn Yahya Al-Zarqali invented a tool that helped sailors navigate. He

This painting of Muslim men in Al-Andalus is from about 1375. It appears on the ceiling of the Alhambra, a Moorish palace in Granada.

also suggested that the orbits of planets were oval rather than circular. It would be another five hundred years before German astronomer Johannes Kepler proved this. Muslim and Jewish cultures interacted in Al-Andalus. Moses Maimonides, a philosopher and physician from Córdoba, was the leading Jewish figure of medieval times.

Al-Andalus also produced much significant architecture. The Great Mosque of Córdoba, which is now a cathedral, is considered one of the most remarkable Islamic buildings anywhere. It is renowned for its massive hall filled with red-and-white striped arches.

Statue of Moses Maimonides in Córdoba. Maimonides wrote a book called *The Guide for the Perplexed*, studying the relationship among religion, philosophy, and science. It was widely influential and is still read today.

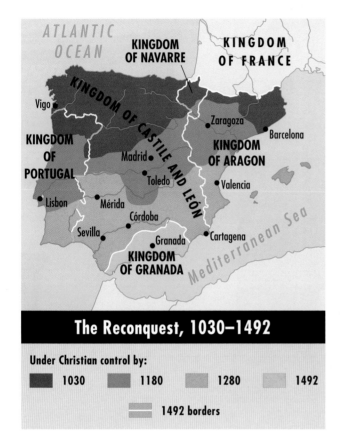

ATLANTIC OCEAN

KINGDOM OF NAVARRE

KINGDOM OF FRANCE

Vigo

KINGDOM OF CASTILE AND LEÓN

Zaragoza

Barcelona

KINGDOM OF PORTUGAL

Madrid

KINGDOM OF ARAGON

Toledo

Valencia

Lisbon

Mérida

Córdoba

Sevilla

Granada

Cartagena

KINGDOM OF GRANADA

Mediterranean Sea

The Reconquest, 1030–1492

Under Christian control by:

■ 1030 ■ 1180 ■ 1280 ■ 1492

■ 1492 borders

The Reconquest

The Moors never gained control of the entire Iberian Peninsula. The northern reaches remained in the hands of Christian groups. Over the centuries, these groups slowly expanded their area of control. This is called the *Reconquista*, or Reconquest.

In 1249, Portugal split off from Spain. By this time, Moorish power in Spain had been reduced to the Kingdom of Granada. In 1492, the last Moorish stronghold surrendered to Christian troops. Moorish rule ended, but Spanish society had been changed by the long interaction of Muslims and Christians, and many Muslims continued to live and work in Spain.

The Era of Exploration

The two most powerful kingdoms on the Iberian Peninsula were Aragon and Castile. In 1469, the two kingdoms were united when Prince Ferdinand of Aragon married Princess Isabella of Castile. Spain was on its way to becoming a world power.

Under Ferdinand and Isabella, Spain began a period of exploration. In 1492, the rulers provided the funds for a jour-

ney by the Italian explorer Christopher Columbus. Columbus sailed west, hoping to find a new route to East Asia, where Spain could trade for valuable spices, silk, and gold. Instead, he stumbled upon the Americas.

King Ferdinand and Queen Isabella funded the voyage of exploration by Christopher Columbus (kneeling) across the Atlantic Ocean.

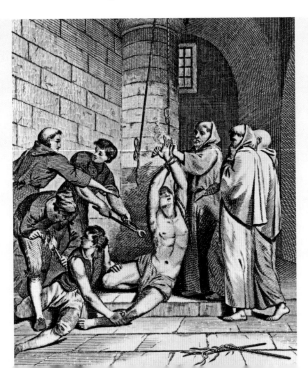

The Spanish Inquisition

Ferdinand and Isabella were called the Catholic Monarchs because of their intense commitment to their faith. They demanded that all Jews become Catholics. The Catholic Monarchs began the Spanish Inquisition, an organized way to find and punish people whose conversion to Catholicism they believed to be insincere. The first inquisition occurred in 1478, and the trials continued until 1834. People brought to trial for failure to follow Catholic rules were sent to prison, tortured, and sometimes killed.

Christopher Columbus kisses the hand of a priest as he departs on his journey. He traveled first to the Canary Islands, where he took on more supplies. From there, he made the five-week journey across the ocean to North America.

Columbus was not the only explorer Spain sent westward. In 1513, Vasco Núñez de Balboa crossed Central America and saw the ocean on the other side. He named the ocean Pacífico, because it was so calm compared to the Atlantic. In 1519, Hernán Cortés arrived in what is now Mexico, and eventually conquered the Aztec Empire.

In the following years, Spain took over all of Central America and moved into South America, where conquistador Francisco Pizarro conquered the Incas of Peru. Spain extended its empire into what is now Florida. All Spanish explorers looked for gold. Cortés and Pizarro found it.

Isabella and Ferdinand had five children. The Spanish

crown arranged marriages for the children, which spread Spain's power into other European countries. One of their grandchildren, Carlos, eventually became the most powerful monarch in Europe. He was King Charles I of Spain and Holy Roman Emperor Charles V. He ruled over much of Europe, the Americas, and other parts of the world.

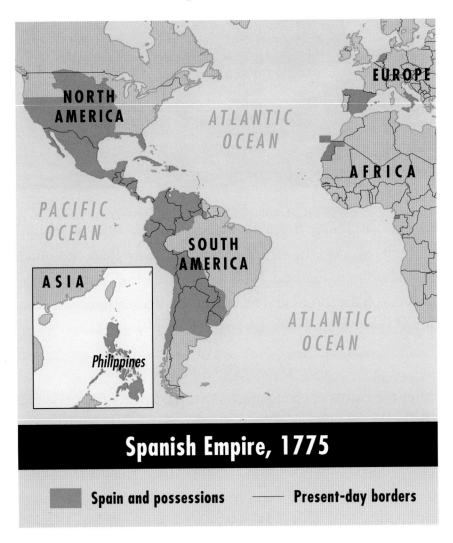

Spanish Empire, 1775

Spain and possessions — Present-day borders

Stormy weather helped the British navy defeat the Spanish Armada.

His son Philip II tried to stamp out the rise of Protestant religions. In 1588, he sent an armada of more than one hundred Spanish ships to England. He hoped to force the Protestant king of England off the throne and replace him with a Catholic. The better-armed British navy easily defeated the Spanish Armada.

The Decline of Spain

After the defeat of the Spanish Armada, Spain's power declined. Philip II's son, Philip III, was not the able leader his father was. He made a mistake when he expelled all the Moors from Spain between 1609 and 1614. Some Moors were scholars, builders, and tradespeople. Without them, Spain's economy struggled. Philip III's son, Philip IV, was also a poor leader, and Spain declined both militarily and politically while he reigned. His heir, Charles II, was the last ruler of this royal line. When he died in 1700, he left no heir to become ruler of Spain. However, he did leave the countries he ruled to a French prince, who became Philip V of Spain.

This set off the War of the Spanish Succession (1701–1714). During this war, British and Austrian armies invaded Spain to try to drive out Philip and replace him with the archduke of Austria. The war diminished Spain's power further.

Philip V (standing at left) reigned as king of Spain for forty-five years.

Spanish, British, and French troops battled in the Pyrenees during the Spanish War of Independence.

In 1808, Napoléon Bonaparte's French army occupied Spain. Spanish rebels, helped by the British, fought back in what Spain calls the War of Independence and the British call the Peninsular War. French armies were finally forced from Spain in 1814, and King Ferdinand VII took the throne under Spain's first democratic constitution.

Ferdinand was not an effective leader, and Spain's global power continued to decline. By the end of his reign, Spain had lost all its colonies except Cuba, the Philippines, Guam, Puerto Rico, and some other islands. Then, as a result of the Spanish-American War of 1898, Spain lost most of its remaining colonies. Its colonial empire was gone.

By the beginning of the twentieth century, average Spaniards had grown tired of the old ways. Workers wanted more power over their lives. With that power came higher pay, better hours, and a political say in their country. They sometimes held strikes, refusing to work until their demands were met. Protests sometimes turned violent.

Striking workers leave a factory in Barcelona in 1910.

In 1923, King Alfonso XIII appointed General Miguel Primo de Rivera prime minister. Many wealthy people approved of him because they thought he would maintain order. Instead, Primo de Rivera installed himself as dictator of Spain. In 1927, with Spain's king Alfonso XIII present, Primo de Rivera officially opened the National Assembly. Though this might have seemed to be a democratic government, Primo de Rivera appointed all the members.

By 1930, Spain and most of the rest of the world were in a deep economic depression. Many people were out of work.

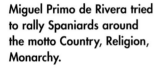
Miguel Primo de Rivera tried to rally Spaniards around the motto Country, Religion, Monarchy.

Businesses closed. Primo de Rivera's government was deeply unpopular, and Alfonso XIII forced him to resign. But the people did not forgive the king for his support of Primo de Rivera, and he faced great opposition.

A soldier raises the Spanish flag after the republicans won the 1931 elections.

The Second Republic

Elections in 1931 showed that Spaniards wanted their nation to be a republic, a form of government where the people, rather than a king or queen, hold the ultimate power. Alfonso suspended the monarchy and left Spain, and the Second Spanish Republic was established.

At first, liberals and moderate socialists ruled in the Second Republic. Women gained the right to vote, and the power of the Catholic Church was diminished. Church organizations could no longer be involved in education. The wealthy, the

Church, and other conservative groups rallied against the government. Meanwhile, the lower classes grew increasingly frustrated that no change was in sight.

Conservatives gained power in the 1933 elections. The following year, some socialists began a revolution that was quickly crushed. Conservative forces were also growing more violent. In 1936, liberals and socialists again gained power. By this time, Spain was starkly divided.

José María Gil Robles (with arm raised) was a leader of conservative Catholic forces during the Second Republic. He was believed to be in favor of bringing back the monarchy.

Civil War

Nationalist forces bombed Barcelona during the Spanish Civil War, leaving many buildings in ruins.

In 1936, rebels under the leadership of General Francisco Franco began a civil war against the elected Spanish government. The two sides during the war were the Left (workers, peasants, union members, and socialists) and the Right, or Nationalists (members of the army, industrial leaders, landowners, monarchists, and the Catholic Church).

The war was bloody, brutal, and destructive. Fighting went on for three years. In the end, the Nationalists won, and Franco became the dictator for the next thirty-six years, until his death in 1975.

By the end of the 1930s, World War II was raging in Europe. Spain was in no position to help either side. Its army

Art Reflects Life

In their art, Spanish painters portrayed the Spanish Civil War and the rise of Fascism, a political philosophy that arose in Europe and included a powerful central government headed by a dictator. Pablo Picasso painted *Guernica* (detail, right) in 1937 in response to the bombing of the city of Guernica by German and Italian forces during the Spanish Civil War. The painting depicts the pain and suffering of civilians during war.

Joan Miró's *Black and Red Series* reveals his emotions after Francisco Franco destroyed so much of

Spain. The etchings feature red signifying blood and the black forms of spider webs, all twisted together and writhing.

was exhausted from three years of civil war. Under Franco, Spain stayed isolated from the rest of the world. People were not allowed to express their political opinions. The Catholic Church grew in power. Trade with outside countries was limited, and the economy suffered.

As Franco aged, he realized that Spain needed to make changes. In 1970, he supported a law making education mandatory for all children from ages six to fourteen. For the first time, Spanish children were required to attend school. In preparation for Spain's future, the previous year, Franco had chosen as his successor Prince Juan Carlos.

Changing Times

Following the death of Franco in 1975, Juan Carlos was crowned king. King Juan Carlos I planned to be monarch in name only. He appointed Adolfo Suárez González prime minister of the government while the country moved through the change from dictatorship to democracy. Juan Carlos called for free elections and the writing of a constitution.

Not all Spaniards were pleased with Spain's liberal government. In 1981, the military tried to overthrow the elected government. Military leaders intent on taking control tried to persuade the army to follow them. The king spoke out, urging the soldiers to stand down. The overthrow was put down, and new elections were held the following year.

General Francisco Franco kept tight control on Spain throughout his long rule.

During these years, Spain developed closer relationships with other nations. The country became a member of the European Union (EU) and the North Atlantic Treaty Organization (NATO). In 1992, Spain hosted the Olympic Summer Games in Barcelona. The country had thoroughly established its position in Europe and the world.

As a member of the EU, Spain's borders were opened to trade with other nations and to easy travel from one country to the next. In 2002, Spain and other countries in the EU gave up their own currencies and began using a single currency called the euro.

A ship moves across the stadium during the opening ceremonies of the Barcelona Olympics.

Supporters of Basque independence attend a protest in 2011.

Spain Today

In recent years, Spain has had to deal with the issue of terrorism. Spain faces terrorist threats from various groups, including Euskadi Ta Askatasuna (ETA) and al-Qaeda. ETA is a Basque organization determined to found a separate Basque nation. The group has used violence to achieve this, killing more than eight hundred people and kidnapping dozens of others. In October 2011, ETA agreed to a cease-fire and an end to its armed activities. Other ETA cease-fires have been broken, however. No one knows how long the current one will last.

Al-Qaeda is a global Islamist terrorist group. It has been involved in bombings and other violent acts around the

A group of Ecuadorian immigrants harvest lettuce in southern Spain. About a half million Ecuadorians live in Spain.

world. On March 11, 2004, bombs exploded in Madrid trains, killing 191 people and injuring around 2,000. It isn't known definitively which group was behind the bombings, though reportedly al-Qaeda claimed to be responsible.

During Franco's rule, few foreigners immigrated to Spain. However, since the country joined the EU, immigrants have been entering, starting as a trickle and then becoming a flood. More than 2.5 million immigrants entered Spain during the period from 2004 to 2010. Since 2000, the number of immigrants in Spain has risen from 2 percent to 12 percent, or 5.6 million people. Most of the immigrant population comes from Morocco and other areas of North Africa, Latin America, or Romania.

In a strong economy, a large immigrant population can be absorbed and provided jobs. But as the economy flounders, jobs disappear. This has been the case in Spain. In 2008, Spain's unemployment rate reached 20 percent. Among immigrants, unemployment reached 30 percent.

By the end of 2011, Spain's economy was on the brink of bankruptcy. Spaniards held elections, and conservative Mariano Rajoy of the Popular Party (PP) was elected prime minister. The following year, the EU bailed out Spanish banks, but the nation's economy remains on shaky ground.

Mariano Rajoy's Popular Party won 53 percent of the seats in the parliament in the 2011 election.

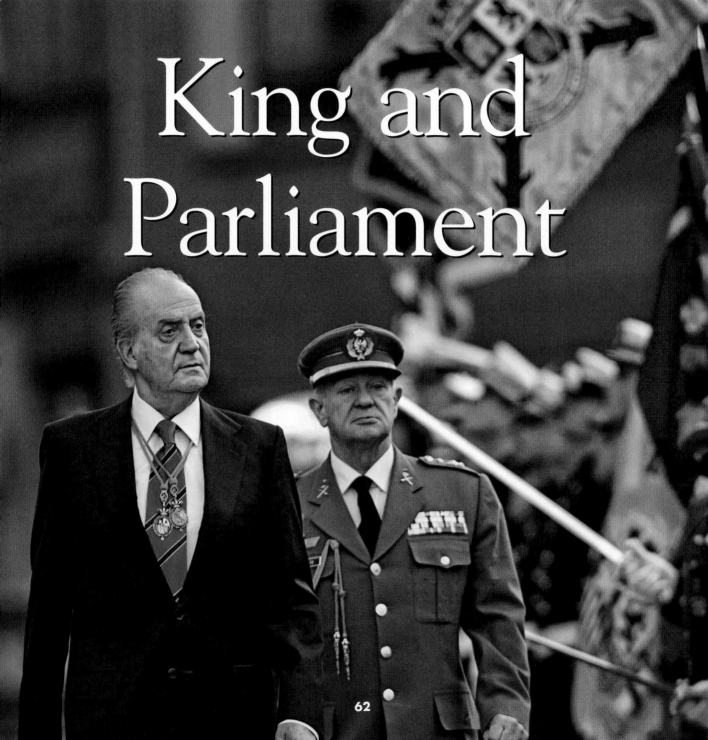

King and Parliament

62

WHEN FRANCISCO FRANCO DIED IN 1975, THIRTY-six years of dictatorship came to an end. Within two days of Franco's death, Juan Carlos was named king. He immediately said that he wanted to establish democracy in Spain. In order for Spain to be a democratic society, with its government elected by the people, it needed a constitution, a document that outlined the organization of the government. In 1978, a constitution was approved.

Spain is a parliamentary monarchy, a country that has a king or queen as its national leader and a government elected by its people. Spain's king is a figurehead, which is a person who represents Spain and its people. He does not set policies or make laws. That job falls to the prime minister, cabinet, and members of the legislature.

The Constitution

The Spanish constitution of 1978 proclaims Spain to be a democratic state and charges the country with ensuring the liberty and equality of its citizens. All Spaniards have the right to vote once they reach eighteen years old. They are protected from unfair arrests and search of their property, and are guaranteed public trials. Spaniards have freedom of religion, speech, and assembly.

Throughout Spain's long history, the Roman Catholic Church and the Spanish army held great power over the people. This new constitution limited that power. No longer would Roman Catholicism be the state religion. And the army's role would be to keep Spain safe during times of war, safeguard borders, and defend the constitution. Only members of the legislature could declare war.

A man votes at a polling station in Barcelona. About 70 percent of Spaniards allowed to vote went to the polls during the 2011 election.

The government includes two houses of parliament, called the Cortes Generales (General Courts). Members of the parliament are chosen by election. Although the constitution established a federal government for Spain, it also recognized the differences that exist from one region to the next. Each region would have specific powers, form a local government, and be responsible for major social programs, such as health care and education.

The Congress of Deputies has 350 members.

Politics

Spain has about eighty-five political parties, but two parties dominate Spanish politics: the Spanish Socialist Workers' Party (PSOE) and the Popular Party (PP). In 2012, eleven parties had representatives in the legislature. Of the smaller parties, the Convergence and Union (CiU) and the United Left have a large number of followers.

Madrid: Spain's Capital City

Madrid is the capital of Spain and its largest city, with an estimated population of 3,273,049 in 2010. It sits along the Manzanares River on the Meseta, in central Spain. People have lived on the site for thousands of years, but the city itself dates back to the ninth century, when a small village was built there. Madrid remained small until Philip II made it the capital in 1561.

Today, Madrid is a thriving, bustling city, the financial and cultural heart of the nation. It is the center of Spain's banking and insurance industries.

At the center of Madrid is a large plaza called the Puerta del Sol (Gateway of the Sun). Busy streets radiate out from this plaza. A tangle of narrow streets surround Plaza Mayor, in the oldest part of the city. Madrid is full of impressive buildings. The Royal Palace is one of the grandest in Europe, with 2,800 rooms.

Madrid also boasts many major museums. The Prado Museum has one of the world's greatest collections of European art. For twentieth-century art, visitors head to the Museo Reina Sofía, which has excellent collections of works by Picasso, Dalí, and other Spanish artists. The National Archaeological Museum displays artifacts from all periods of history on the Iberian Peninsula and has a replica of Altamira Cave.

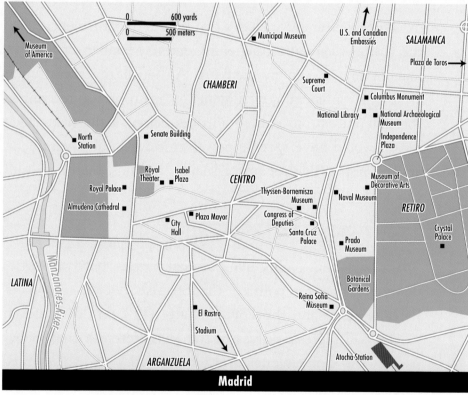

In general elections, the PSOE and the PP earn the vast majority of votes and, therefore, the most seats in the legislature. The party that wins the most seats forms a government. That means its main leader becomes prime minister, and its lesser leaders become members of the prime minister's cabinet of advisers. In Spain, voters do not choose specific people in an election. Instead, they vote for the political party they want to represent their district.

When no party holds a majority of seats, several parties band together to form a coalition. If the PP held 130 seats, the CiU held 45 seats, and a third party held 6 seats, those three parties could pool their members to create a majority of seats in Congress with 181. Leaders consider the plans and policies of all parties in a coalition when making new laws.

José Luis Rodríguez Zapatero (in brown) greets supporters at a rally. He served as prime minister until the PSOE lost the election in 2011.

Spain's parliament is called the General Courts. It is made up of two houses, the Congress of Deputies and the Senate. The Congress of Deputies has 350 members who are elected every four years. The Senate has 264 members, 208 of whom are elected, while the other 56 are appointed by regional legislatures. Senators serve four-year terms.

The Congress of Deputies is the more powerful of the two houses. It approves all laws. The Senate reviews laws and may

SPAIN'S NATIONAL GOVERNMENT

Executive Branch

KING

PRIME MINISTER

CABINET

Legislative Branch

| CONGRESS OF DEPUTIES (350 MEMBERS) | SENATE (264 MEMBERS) |

Judicial Branch

SUPREME COURT

| NATIONAL HIGH COURT | CONSTITUTIONAL COURT |

HIGH COURTS

REGIONAL COURTS

make additions or changes, but the Congress has the power to refuse changes and approve laws despite opinions in the Senate.

A new building was added to the Spanish Senate complex in Madrid in 1987.

Executive Branch

In November 2011, Spain held a general election, and power shifted from the PSOE to the PP. The leader of the Popular Party, Mariano Rajoy, became the new prime minister. The prime minister appoints various members of his party to positions in his cabinet of advisers. These ministers are responsible for specific areas within the government. For example, the Minister of Defense deals with the army, navy, and air force, and all military matters.

Ministers know that their jobs are temporary. If citizens become dissatisfied with the government or it becomes impossible to pass necessary laws, the prime minister may call for a vote of confidence in the Congress. If Congress votes that it does not have confidence in the current government, a new election may be held.

The Justice System

The most powerful body in the Spanish justice system is the Supreme Court. The head of the Supreme Court is called the president and is elected by the General Council of the Judiciary, a group of twenty justices. The king officially appoints the president of the Supreme Court. The Supreme Court is the last resort for legal cases. It determines if cases heard in lower courts followed Spain's laws.

The National High Court oversees trials of criminal cases that are either national or involve more than one region.

Mariano Rajoy

Mariano Rajoy (1955–) is a Conservative politician and leader of the Popular Party. He was born in the Galicia region of northern Spain. He attended the University of Santiago de Compostela, where he studied law. In the 1980s, he began serving in the local government. Rajoy was first elected to the Congress of Deputies in 1986. In the years after, he served as minister of public administration, minister of education and culture, and minister of the interior. In 2011, his party came to power, and Rajoy became prime minister.

This court also hears civil cases that deal with federal issues, such as an issue dealing with a nationwide labor dispute. There are several other high courts that hear certain kinds of appeals, often involving the government or government officials. Regional courts deal with local criminal and civil issues. Lower courts include city criminal courts; juvenile courts, which handle crimes by children under age eighteen; and courts of peace, which deal with minor civil cases, divorces, wills, and property deeds.

The constitution of 1978 also established the Constitutional Court. This court evaluates potential laws to make sure they do not take away the rights of citizens or regional governments.

The Spanish Supreme Court meets in a building that was originally a convent, a place where nuns live.

Spain's Flag

Spain's national flag features three horizontal bands. The top and bottom bands are red, and between them is a broader yellow band. In the yellow band is the Spanish coat of arms, which shows symbols of the historic kingdoms of Spain. The two columns framing the coat of arms represent the Pillars of Hercules, the two rocky peaks that guard the entrance to the Mediterranean Sea.

Autonomous Communities

Many years ago, Spain was made up of several different kingdoms. Each kingdom had its own ruler, customs, language, and lifestyle. When the new constitution was written, the government wanted the old regions to be able to keep their customs and celebrations. As a result, the constitution divided Spain into seventeen autonomous communities. Autonomous means being independent or capable of self-rule. These communities have their own governments with executive, legislative, and judicial branches, just like Spain's federal government. The governments of the autonomous communities are responsible for health care, education, culture, urban and rural development, and universities. More than half of the people who work for the government in Spain work for autonomous communities.

Autonomous communities represent people with a common history or culture. For example, although Castilian Spanish is the official language of Spain, people who live in Catalonia also speak Catalan, their regional language. The autonomous com-

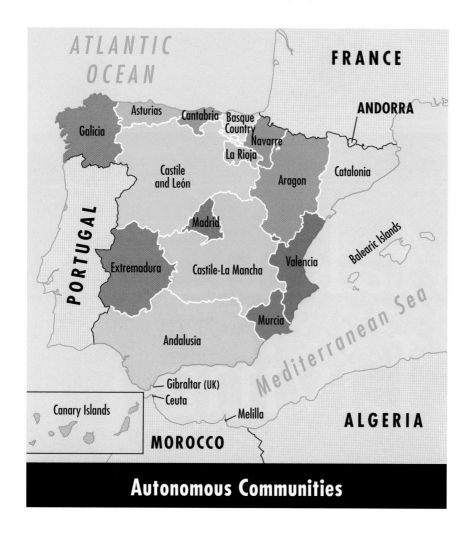

ATLANTIC OCEAN

FRANCE

ANDORRA

Galicia

Asturias

Cantabria

Basque Country

Navarre

La Rioja

Castile and León

Aragon

Catalonia

Madrid

PORTUGAL

Extremadura

Castile-La Mancha

Valencia

Balearic Islands

Murcia

Andalusia

Mediterranean Sea

Gibraltar (UK)

Ceuta

Canary Islands

Melilla

ALGERIA

MOROCCO

Autonomous Communities

munity of Catalonia recognizes Catalan as an official language. Another feature of autonomous communities is local holidays. The community of Andalusia, for example, has a special regional holiday called Día de Andalusia.

Spain's National Anthem

The Spanish national anthem is *"La marcha real"* ("The Royal March"). The anthem has no lyrics. The hymn was Spain's official anthem from 1770 to 1931, and then became the national anthem again in 1939.

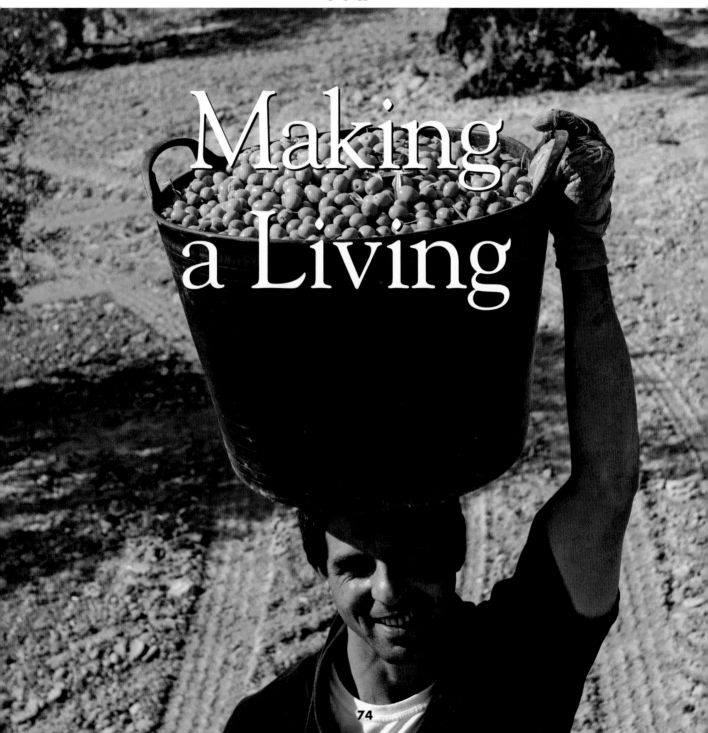

Making a Living

SPAIN'S ECONOMY IS LARGELY BASED ON SERVICES. About 71 percent of all workers are employed in service industries. Service industries include banking, tourism, and restaurants. Another one-quarter of Spanish workers are employed in industry. Only 4 percent of workers are involved in farming.

Opposite: **A man harvests olives in Extremadura, in western Spain. The nation produces about 8.8 million tons (8 million metric tons) of olives every year.**

Fruits of the Land

Many parts of Spain are too dry or mountainous to easily grow crops. But since the 1970s, Spain made its land more productive by improving irrigation. Cereals are Spain's largest crops, although the country's wheat and barley production is lower than that of other European countries.

Spain's most significant crops are olives, oranges, and grapes for wine production. Some olives are consumed as snacks and used as ingredients in recipes, but most are used to produce olive oil. Spain produces more olives than any other country, and more than twice as many as Italy produces. Oranges are grown in regions along the Mediterranean coast. More than 80 percent of the oranges Europe produces come from Spain

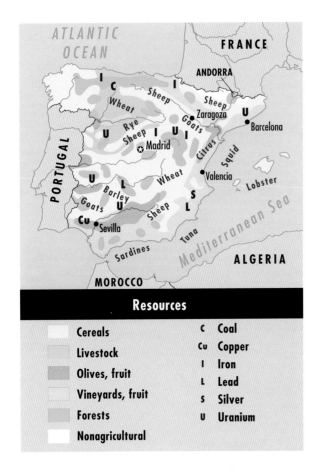

Resources		
Cereals	C	Coal
Livestock	Cu	Copper
Olives, fruit	I	Iron
Vineyards, fruit	L	Lead
Forests	S	Silver
Nonagricultural	U	Uranium

and Italy. Spain is also a leader in wine grapes, producing about 6.6 million tons (6 metric tons) a year. It is one of the top five countries in wine grape production.

Spain harvests many other products as well, including cotton, tobacco, sugar beets, beans, lentils, and chickpeas. Apple, plum, and apricot orchards dot the southern coast.

Inland, small farms raise livestock. Hogs are the most important meat product, and smoked or cured hams are top sellers throughout Spanish markets. Cattle are raised in north and northwest regions that include Galicia and Cantabria, while Merino sheep, known for their fine wool, are grown in the northern region of Castile.

Jamón

If Spain were to have a national dish, it could be ham. Nearly every bar and restaurant sells at least one type of ham. The government has specific regulations regarding how ham is bred, fed, slaughtered, and prepared. *Jamón Serrano* comes from white pigs. *Jamón Trevélez* is cured at a minimum altitude of 3,900 feet (1,200 m). And *jamón Ibérico de bellota* is ham from pigs fed exclusively on acorns.

A Spanish fisher unloads his catch onto a dock.

Fishing

Spain's two largest fishing ports are Vigo and Coruña on the Atlantic coast. Spain has heavily fished its own waters, and commercial fishers must venture farther and farther into the ocean in order to bring home a catch.

Commercial fishers haul in shrimps, crabs, and lobsters. They catch mackerel, tuna, and cod. Octopus and squid are popular seafood for tapas.

Mining

Coal is one of Spain's most important mining products. In 2010, the country produced 11,478,963 tons (10,413,540 metric tons) of coal, 7 percent less than the previous year.

Since 1989, coal production has gone down every year. Spain produces about 154,000,000 tons (140,000,000 metric tons) of iron ore every year. Production is increasing for copper, a valuable metal used in making pipes and electrical wire.

Manufacturing

One of Spain's major industries is textiles and apparel. Cotton and wool, both natural fibers that are produced in Spain, are woven into cloth and turned into high fashion. Barcelona and Madrid are fashion centers, where internationally known designers turn out everything from expensive jeans to evening gowns.

Steel and iron are also produced in Spain. They provide the materials for making ships, automobiles, tools, and medical equipment. Spain is also a major producer and exporter of chemicals, including fertilizers and medicines.

What Spain Grows, Makes, and Mines

Agriculture

Olives (2009)	7,900,000 metric tons
Grapes (2009)	5,995,300 metric tons
Oranges (2010)	3,453,000 metric tons

Manufacturing

Pig iron (2010)	3,995,000 metric tons
Steel (2010)	18,400,000 metric tons
Motor vehicles (2011)	2,353,682 units

Mining (2010)

Iron ore	140,000,000 metric tons
Coal	10,413,540 metric tons
Copper	7,100 metric tons

Services

Tourism is the biggest service industry in Spain, and Spain has the fifth-largest tourism market in the world. The main tourist season is summer, when people from all over Europe flock to Spain's sandy beaches. The beautiful Spanish coastline, rugged mountains, and warm islands attract visitors by the millions. Tourism brings in fifty-three million visitors each year and accounts for $81 billion of the Spanish economy. Tourism-related service jobs include travel agents who plan trips, hotel workers who provide lodging, and restaurant workers

What Does It Cost?

Here are 2011 prices of grocery items in Spain and their U.S. dollar equivalents:

Item	Price in Euros (€)	Price in U.S. Dollars ($)
2.2 pounds (1 kg) apples	1.15	1.50
6-pack of yogurt	2.99	3.93
11 pounds (5 kg) potatoes	1.65	2.17
11 ounces (300 g) Havarti cheese	2.69	3.54
2.2 pounds (1 kg) chicken breasts	6.25	8.22
1 loaf of French bread	0.59	0.78
5.5 ounces (150 g) sliced ham	3.35	4.41

who feed hungry tourists. Taxi drivers, scuba instructors, and deep-sea fishing guides are all service workers.

Finance is another major service industry in Spain. This industry includes bankers, stockbrokers, and insurance agents. Madrid and Barcelona are Spain's major financial centers.

As the years go by, Spain's citizens are living longer and longer. An aging population means an increased demand for health care. Spain has a thriving market for doctors, nurses, dentists, and medical specialists. The country's health care system is ranked the seventh best in the world.

Economic Ups and Downs

Spain is one of twenty-seven nations in the European Union (EU). One of the fundamental ideas of the EU is that there are no tariffs—taxes on imports and exports—among member countries. Under Franco's rule, Spain charged high tariffs on imports from other countries. This allowed Spanish producers to charge high prices for their goods. Under the EU, Spanish goods must compete evenly against other countries' products. For many years, Spain did well. By 2005, Spain's economy was growing faster than that of other EU countries. In 2011, Spain had the twelfth-largest economy in the world and the fifth largest in the European Union.

But between 2008 and 2011 Spain's economy tumbled. Spain was buying more goods from other countries than it was selling. Personal debt among families exploded, and unemployment reached an alarming 20 percent. In 2011, an election changed the leadership of the country. The new prime minister, Mariano Rajoy, won because he promised to deal with the economic crisis. The problems are deep, however, so it is a difficult task.

Coming and Going

Spain exports machinery, motor vehicles, fruits and vegetables, grains, and medicines. The country imports other machinery, oil products, foods, consumer goods, and chemicals. Major trading partners are members of the European Union. Exports head to France, Germany, Portugal, Italy, and the United Kingdom. Imports come from Germany, France, Italy, China, the Netherlands, and the United Kingdom.

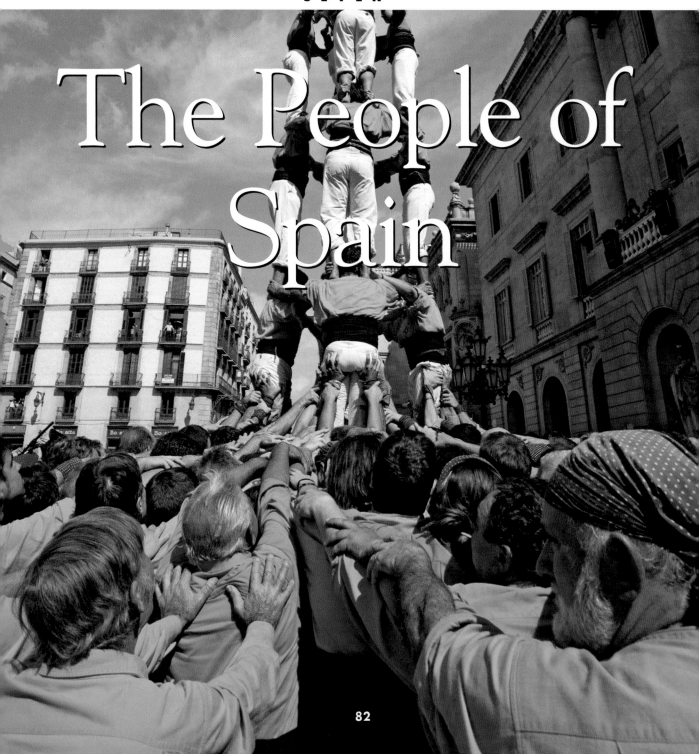

The People of Spain

ALIZE AND KEMINA ARE BASQUE TEENS WHO come from very different backgrounds. Alize lives in Bilbao, a city of 354,000 people. Daughter of a shipbuilding executive, Alize goes to secondary school and plans to attend university in Barcelona. To prepare for her move, Alize has been studying Catalan, the language of Barcelona, with a tutor. She takes a full science-based schedule at school, followed by two hours of tutoring and then homework and family time. Alize wants to become a chemist.

Kemina has a totally different lifestyle. She lives on a sheep farm in the foothills of the Pyrenees. She attends school from 9:00 a.m. to 2:00 p.m. Before and after school, she helps her family with the many chores that keep a family farm running. In early spring, the lambs are born. In late spring, the sheep need to be sheared. Everyone works hard year-round. During lambing and shearing, Kemina often misses school.

Opposite: **Building human towers is a traditional activity at festivals in Catalonia. It dates back to the 1700s.**

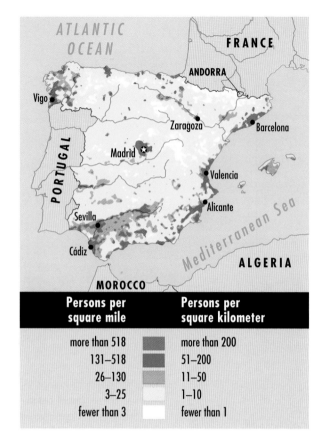

Persons per square mile		Persons per square kilometer
more than 518		more than 200
131–518		51–200
26–130		11–50
3–25		1–10
fewer than 3		fewer than 1

Population of major cities (2010 est.)

Madrid	3,273,049
Barcelona	1,673,075
Valencia	809,267
Sevilla	705,107
Zaragoza	701,090

She gets no weekends off and has barely enough time to do her homework, but she would not change her life one bit. Her family has lived in the same place for more than thirty generations.

Population

Spain is a mixture of dense cities and large stretches of land with few people. The population, 46,754,784, ranks 27th in the world. Seventy-seven percent of Spaniards live in cities. Cities such as Madrid and Barcelona sprawl out into crowded suburbs. Madrid has a population of 3,273,049 within the city and another two and a half million outside the city. Similarly, Barcelona's population more than doubles when suburbs are included in the count.

The Meseta and the surrounding mountains tend to have the lowest population density, despite Madrid's central location. Most of central Spain has between 3 and 65 people per square mile (1 and 25 people per sq km). In small sections of the Pyrenees to the north, the population is even sparser.

A Mix of People

Spain served as a stepping-stone between Europe and Africa for centuries. Throughout its history it has been conquered and influenced by cultures from both Europe and Africa. Spain

A Chinese man bicycles through Barcelona. Chinese immigrants have been coming to Spain since the 1920s.

entered a period of relative isolation for several hundred years after it expelled the Moors and the Jews. This changed after World War II ended, when Spain began exporting its workers. Cheap Spanish labor was needed throughout Europe to rebuild cities, roads, and railroads. Then, as Spain became more industrialized, it did not have enough workers. By the beginning of the twenty-first century, people immigrated to Spain in large numbers to find work. They came from other EU countries, as well as from North Africa, Latin America, and Asia.

North Africans make up about 1 percent of Spain's population. Most come from Morocco or Algeria. Large numbers of immigrants have also come from Romania, Ecuador, Colombia, and China.

One ethnic group that is represented in Spain is the Roma, or gypsies, called *gitanos* in Spain. Historically, Roma have been travelers, picking up jobs as they move from place to place. Some of Spain's Roma population still moves often, in search of work or better weather, while others have settled in cities. Large communities of Roma are found in Murcia, Almería, Granada, Barcelona, and Madrid. Estimates for Spain's

Roma women sell flowers in Sevilla. More than ten million Roma live in Europe.

Roma population vary from seven hundred thousand to almost a million.

The Basque people have long lived in northern Spain's rugged Pyrenees. Euskara, the language of the Basques, is not related to other modern European languages. About two million Basque people live in Spain, making up about 5 percent of Spain's population. Some Basques believe that they should have their own

Spanish Names

Spanish last names differ from English names. Tennis player Arantxa Sánchez Vicario has two last names, or surnames. Sánchez is her father's surname, and Vicario is her mother's name. Many Spaniards use both names, such as poet Federico García Lorca. Others, like tennis player Rafael Nadal Parera, use only their father's name.

Names like Sánchez and Rodríguez follow the same pattern as names like McWilliams or Johannson. Mc- and -son both mean "son of." Often, the -ez suffix on Spanish surnames means the same thing. Sánchez means "son of Sancho"; Rodríguez means "son of Rodrigo."

nation, separate from Spain. Some extreme Basque nationalists have even used violence to try to achieve this.

Basques have their own traditions and customs, including games, traditional clothing, music, and sports. Pelota is the

Basque men playing pelota. In some versions of pelota, players hit the ball with their hands, while in other versions, they use rackets.

national sport of the Basques. It is similar to tennis but played with bare hands, wooden rackets, or specially designed baskets. Pelota is a fast-paced game—a ball can whip across the court at speeds up to 185 miles per hour (300 kph). Fiestas, or festivals, are common, and activities revolve around traditional Basque skills such as log cutting, bale tossing, tug-of-war, and sheepdog handling. No Basque fiesta would be complete without dancing. The Basque culture has more than four hundred traditional dances.

Language

Some signs in Catalonia are written in both Castilian Spanish (top) and Catalan (middle).

Spain's national language is Castilian Spanish, and most Spaniards can speak Castilian. That does not mean, however, that Castilian is their primary language. Regional autonomous communities have a second official language. These include Catalan, Euskara, and Galician, which are taught in regions where the languages are in use. A student in Palma (on Majorca) or in Barcelona, for example, would study Catalan.

Catalan is similar to Spanish. It is spoken in Catalonia and other parts of eastern Spain, as well as in parts of France and Sardinia. Nine to ten million people in Spain speak Catalan.

Euskara, the language of the Basques, is believed to be one of the oldest languages in Europe. Speakers of Euskara live on both sides of the Pyrenees, in Spain and France. It is estimated that between six hundred thousand and three million people speak Euskara.

Galician, or Gallego, is the language of the northwestern corner of Spain. Some linguists, people who study languages, claim that Portuguese evolved from Galician. About 90 percent of Galicia's 2.8 million residents speak Galician.

Education

It is the first week of September, and María is heading off to baccalaureate school. This is a school for seventeen- and eighteen-year-old students who plan to go to university. This is the first year that María is attending a public school. Like

Reading Castilian Spanish

Spanish vowels have only one sound. The same is true of most Spanish consonants, except for the letters c, g, and ll.

a	"ah" as in *far*
e	"ay" as in *hay*
i	"ee" as in *see*
o	"oh" as in *solo*
u	"oo" as in *flu*
ñ	"nyuh" as in *canyon*
ll	"yuh" as in *million*
c before *e* or *i*	"th" as in *theme*
c before *a*, *o*, or *u*	"k" as in *car*
g before *e* or *i*	"ch" as in *loch*
z	"thuh" as in *thunder*

How Do You Say...?

Here are a few common words and phrases in Castilian Spanish:

buenos días	good morning
buenas tardes	good afternoon
adiós	good-bye
¿Cómo está usted?	How are you?
Muy bien.	I'm fine.
sí	yes
no	no
perdón	excuse me
gracias	thank you
de nada	you're welcome
¿Puede usted ayudarme?	Can you help me?

30 percent of Spanish schoolchildren, María has previously attended a Catholic school. She has always worn a school uniform, but now she is free to wear what she wants.

The traditional school year runs from September to the end of June, with plenty of holidays during the year. Students get a long break at Christmas, Easter, and during the summer. There are also days off for national and local holidays, and additional time off between primary and secondary school. School hours may be from 9:00 a.m. to 5:00 p.m. with a two-hour break for lunch, or 9:00 a.m. to 2:00 p.m. without lunch.

The Spanish government funds schooling for children from ages three to eighteen. Preschool is for ages three to five, and is voluntary. Primary school is for children six to twelve. Secondary school educates children twelve through eighteen. Both primary and secondary school are required for all chil-

dren. Primary school students study Spanish and the regional language, math, physical education, arts and crafts, and either English or French. They also study *conocimiento del medio* (knowledge of the environment), a combination of history, biology, geography, and local culture.

Spain offers two types of secondary schooling. Students who intend to go to university take academic classes. Other students receive a vocational education, which trains them to be trade professionals such as clerks, electricians, and computer repair people. Students in academic secondary schools study the usual subjects of math, science, history, and Spanish and the regional language. Many students also study English or French. Most Spaniards speak two or more languages.

A professor explains an experiment at the University of the Basque Country.

Languages in Spain	
Castilian Spanish	74%
Catalan	17%
Galician	7%
Basque	2%

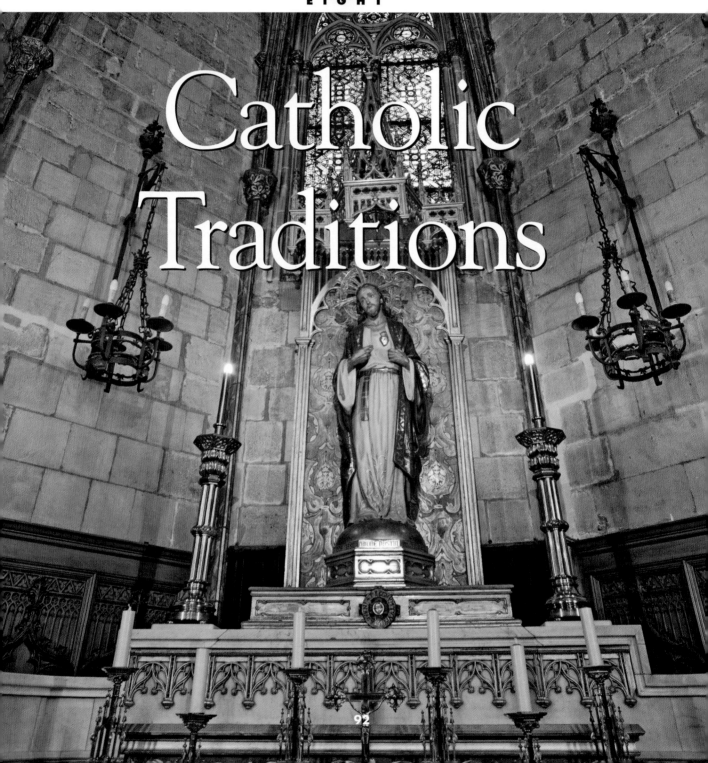

Catholic Traditions

CARLOS AND MARTINA HAVE A HEALTHY BABY
girl. By tradition, she has been named Daniela Lucía after
Martina's mother. The baby is a few weeks old, and plans are
underway for the child's baptism. Carlos's brother and his wife
will be the godparents. Even if the family is not religious, baptism is still an important part of life. The parents hold a large
party, inviting family and friends.

Roman Catholicism

Since the time of Ferdinand and Isabella, Roman Catholics
had tremendous power in Spanish politics. The government
paid the salaries of priests, built churches, and supported
Catholic schools.

The end of Franco's dictatorship saw a change in the
church's control over Spain. The new constitution declared
that Spain would not have an official religion. All Spaniards
had the right to pursue the religion of their choice.

Religion in Spain

Roman Catholic	94%
Protestant	3%
Muslim	2.5%
Jewish	0.1%

Santiago de Compostela

The city of Santiago de Compostela is in Galicia, in northwestern Spain. Catholic pilgrims have been traveling to the city since the Middle Ages, around fifteen hundred to five hundred years ago. They walk across France and Spain to visit the beautiful Cathedral of Santiago de Compostela. It became a pilgrimage site because it is said to be the burial place of St. James, one of the twelve apostles who followed Jesus and was killed in Jerusalem in 44 CE.

Parts of the cathedral date back to the eleventh century, but it stands on the site of a ninth-century church. The ninth-century crypt of St. James lies beneath the cathedral's altar. Throughout the centuries, the church has seen many additions. The Doorway of Glory features statues of apostles and prophets, which were sculpted during the twelfth century.

In recent years, Spaniards have moved away from the church in increasing numbers. Although 94 percent of Spain's population is considered Catholic, 54 percent say they never or rarely attend church. Another 15 percent go to church several times a year, 10 percent attend monthly, and 19 percent attend every week.

Although many Spaniards no longer attend church, they still have their children baptized, have them participate in other Catholic ceremonies, and have them attend Catholic schools.

Catholic Holidays

Because so much of the population is Catholic, schools and businesses are typically closed on Catholic holidays.

The Christmas season is a two-week holiday that begins on Nochebuena—Christmas Eve—and ends on Día de Reyes—Three Kings Day, January 6. Children receive gifts on Three Kings Day. They put straw or barley in their shoes to "feed the camels" that are said to have carried the three wise men to see Jesus in Bethlehem.

King Juan Carlos looks on as his grandson Felipe Juan is baptized.

Religious Holidays

Three Kings Day	January 6
Maundy (Holy) Thursday	last Thursday before Easter
Good Friday	last Friday before Easter
Easter Sunday	March or April
Assumption	August 15
All Saints' Day	November 1
Immaculate Conception	December 8
Christmas	December 25

Easter is a more serious holiday, celebrating when Jesus is said to have come back from the dead. The Easter season includes another long holiday from work and school. The week before Easter is Semana Santa, or Holy Week. The cus-

A boy collects wax from a candle during a Holy Week procession.

toms of Semana Santa go back to the sixteenth century. They developed from a need to present Jesus's last days in a way that all people could understand. Today, festivities begin on Palm Sunday and end on Easter Monday. Men move through the streets in cloaks with pointed, cone-shaped caps. The robes bring to mind the medieval days and remind people of the need to show sorrow for committing sins.

All Saints' Day, November 1, is a day for remembering the dead. In many households, the day is celebrated with a meal, followed by roasted chestnuts and small almond cakes. In some homes, families eat roasted sweet potatoes along with chestnuts. In villages, people might sit around bonfires and

Processions snake through the streets of Spanish cities during Semana Santa.

The Red Fortress

The Alhambra was a Moorish palace and fortress built in the fourteenth century, which protected the city of Granada. *Alhambra* comes from the words "the red" in Arabic. The building probably got its name from the color of its bricks. The Alhambra features remarkable mosaics and architectural details. The Hall of the Abencerrajes has a honeycomb of blue, brown, red, and gold in small domes. The Patio of the Lions is a courtyard with open corridors supported by 124 marble columns and decorated with blue, yellow, and gold tiles. Twelve statues of lions surround the fountain in the patio's center.

tell ghost stories. Families visit the tombs of their dead relatives and decorate them with flowers.

Islam

The Moors came to Spain in 711 and eventually gained control of much of the land. The Moors were Muslim, and their rule in Spain lasted for nearly eight hundred years. After the Moors lost power, the heritage of Islam remained in Spain in the form of mosques, other buildings, and artwork. By 1616, most Spanish Muslims had either been killed or forced from the country.

After the end of Franco's reign in 1975, religious tolerance increased in Spain and Muslims once again began to move there. Today, more than 1.5 million Muslims live in Spain. Most came from North Africa, while others are former

Catholics who have converted to Islam. Today, Spain has more than four hundred mosques where Muslims go to pray.

Judaism

Jews lived in Spain for centuries, until the rise of Ferdinand and Isabella in the late 1400s. In 1492, most Jews were forced from Spain, but some remained. During World War II, Spain allowed more than twenty-five thousand Jews to enter the country to escape Nazi persecution. Groups of Jews settled in Barcelona, Valencia, and Madrid. Today, between thirty thousand and fifty thousand Jews live in Spain, mostly in major cities. The Córdoba Synagogue dates back to 1315, and is one of the last three remaining ancient synagogues in Spain.

Muslims praying at a mosque in Madrid. When praying, Muslims always face in the direction of Mecca, Saudi Arabia, the holiest city in Islam.

Arts and Sports

VELAZQUEZ

100

E LANA'S ART CLASS IS SKETCHING IN THE PRADO Museum. As an art student, seventeen-year-old Elana appreciates the opportunity to spend time with the great masters of Spanish art. Today, class is studying portraits, and what could be better than the paintings by Diego Velázquez, including his portrait of Doña Antonia and her son Don Luis. This semester is all about baroque art. Next semester, Elana plans to study the great modern artist Pablo Picasso at the Centro de Arte Reina Sofía, another of Madrid's fine art museums.

Elana's brother, Hernán, is interested in sports. He plays tennis. Like many teens, he idolizes Rafael Nadal, the world's number one tennis player and a hero in Spain. Hernán goes to a tennis academy founded by former tennis players Emilio Sánchez Vicario and Sergio Casal. He attends school at the Schiller International School, located at the tennis academy, and practices tennis daily.

Opposite: **A statue of Diego Velázquez sits in front of the Prado Museum in Madrid.**

A self-portrait by Francisco de Goya. He was renowned for painting portraits that revealed the true nature of the subject.

Visual Arts

Spain has a long tradition of world-renowned painters. One of the finest portrait painters of the time, Diego Velázquez (1599–1660) was the court artist of King Philip IV and painted many members of the royal family. El Greco (1541–1614), whose real name was Doménikos Theotokópoulos, was born in Greece. He moved to Toledo, Spain, as a young man. He is known for painting strangely elongated figures and dramatic backgrounds. His greatest works include *The Disrobing of Christ* and *View of Toledo*. Francisco de Goya (1746–1828) served as a court painter. His masterpieces include the painting *The Clothed Maja* and a series of prints called *The Disasters of War*. Many of Velázquez's, El Greco's, and Goya's greatest works are on display in the Prado Museum in Madrid.

During the twentieth century, Spaniards were leaders in the art world. Pablo Picasso was one of the greatest artists of that century. Salvador Dalí was the principal artist of the surrealist movement, an artistic style that stretches even the most vivid imaginations and produces dreamlike images in paintings. One of his best-known works, *The Persistence of Memory*, depicts melting clocks. Another renowned painter, Joan Miró, made colorful, creative works with mixed media.

Theater

The earliest forms of theater in Spain were religious plays presented on saints' days or at church festivals. The plays featured both human and supernatural characters that represented good and evil and saints and sinners.

From these simple plays emerged the golden age of Spanish drama. The star of the golden age was Lope Félix de Vega Carpio (1562–1635), known as Lope de Vega. He wrote about

Master Painter

Pablo Picasso (1881–1973) was a painter, sculptor, and printmaker considered by many to be the greatest artist of the twentieth century. He was certainly one of the most influential. Picasso helped found the cubist movement. In cubism, artists depict objects from a variety of viewpoints at the same time. Endlessly inventive, he also introduced collage into modern art and worked in styles ranging from classical to surrealist. Among Picasso's most famous works are *The Old Guitarist* and *Guernica*. Picasso said, "Art is a lie that makes us realize truth."

800 full-length plays, 470 of which have survived. Some are still presented in theaters. These include *Punishment Without Vengeance* and *The Knight of Olmedo*.

The golden age ended with another brilliant playwright, Pedro Calderón de la Barca (1600–1681). Calderón de la Barca's best-known play is *Life Is a Dream*, which focuses on the battle between free will and fate.

Music

In Spain music is closely linked to dance. Traditional Spanish music features guitars, drums, tambourines, and castanets, which are shell-shaped objects that are clicked together. The rhythms and themes change from region to region. Andalusia, in southern Spain, is the home of flamenco, a fiery music and dance. The sounds of the Basque country are the accordion, the tambourine, and the *txistu*—a flutelike pipe. In Castile, classical music features the delicate rhythms of dances such as the *jota* and the *fandango*.

Spain has produced several world-renowned opera singers. Generally considered the world's greatest opera singer, Plácido Domingo has a powerful, ringing voice. He has given concerts all around the world. He is also a conductor and is currently working with the Los Angeles Opera. José Carreras is best known for performances in operas by Verdi and Puccini. Together, Domingo, Carreras, and Italy's Luciano Pavarotti made recordings and performed in concerts as the Three Tenors.

Today's Spanish teens listen to a full range of rock and roll, rap, techno, and pop bands, such as Amaral, El Canto del

Loco, Pereza, and La Quinta Estación. The group Chambao mixes pop with Spanish folk music. Solo artists, such as David Bisbal, Merche, and Soraya Arnelas, top the charts with hit tunes. Teens do appreciate music from all around the world, and are just as likely to be listening to Coldplay and Beyoncé as to homegrown musicians like Mago de Oz.

A flamenco dancer twirls and clicks her heels to the rhythm of the music.

Literature

From the days of *Cantar de mío Cid*, the epic poem of Spain's military hero El Cid, Spanish writers have been creating clever, entertaining, world-class literature. One of Spain's earliest novels is also one of its greatest. Miguel de Cervantes published

Mecano

Mecano is a Madrid band that formed in the 1980s and became Spain's first international chart-topping music group. They play acoustic pop rock blended with the rhythms of salsa, flamenco, and tango. With more than twenty-five million albums sold worldwide, Mecano is the Spanish band with the greatest sales. Their hits include "*La fuerza del destino*" ("The Force of Destiny") and "*Mujer contra mujer*" ("Woman Against Woman"). The band broke up in the 1990s, but in recent years they have released new compilations of their work.

Don Quixote in two parts, in 1605 and 1615. The humorous novel tells of the adventures of an aging knight. The novel was a huge success and was quickly translated into English. It remains one of the most widely read Spanish novels.

Five Spanish writers have received the Nobel Prize in Literature: José Echegaray (1904), Jacinto Benavente (1922), Juan Ramón Jiménez (1956), Vicente Aleixandre (1977), and Camilo José Cela (1989). Echegaray and Benavente were playwrights, and Jiménez and Aleixandre were poets. Cela is noted for novels and short stories rich with intense prose. His writings often explore humankind's basic weaknesses.

Spanish poetry often concerns love, religion, heroism, and death. The *romancero* is a type of folk ballad that was popular in the era of Ferdinand and Isabella. Romanceros honored courage, war, and heroics. Many of the early romanceros were legends sung by troubadours as they traveled from town to town.

Modern poets include Antonio Machado and Federico García Lorca. In 1912, Machado published *Fields of Castile*, a collection of poems about the beauty of Spain's Castile region. Most of his later poems explore the themes of death or the common habits of everyday Spaniards.

At the Movies

Spanish movies draw crowds to the theaters in Spain, Mexico, and other Spanish-speaking countries. Several Spanish actors have also made a name for themselves in English-language films. Penélope Cruz has been appearing in television and movies since she was sixteen years old. She has been nominated for and won many acting awards for films such as *Volver* and *Nine*, and she won an Academy Award for Best Supporting Actress for her performance in the film *Vicky Cristina Barcelona*. Cruz's husband, Javier Bardem, is also an Academy Award–winning Spanish actor. Spain's Antonio

Federico García Lorca

Federico García Lorca (1898–1936), born in Granada, Spain, had a significant impact on the literature of Spain in the twentieth century. As a dramatist, García Lorca is known for *Blood Wedding* and *The House of Bernarda Alba*. As a poet, he is remembered for a collection of poems called *Gypsy Ballads*, which used startling imagery to bring to life the world of the Roma. García Lorca was assassinated during the Spanish Civil War, but no trace of his body has ever been found.

Penélope Cruz (left) has appeared in several of Pedro Almodóvar's (right) films, including *All About My Mother.*

Banderas has appeared in many English-language movies, including *The Mambo Kings* and *Philadelphia*. He also gave voice to the Puss in Boots character in the Shrek movies.

All three actors have appeared in movies written and directed by Pedro Almodóvar. He makes movies filled with color, drama, and music. Almodóvar won the Academy Award for Best Foreign Language Film for *All About My Mother* (1999). His 2002 film *Talk to Her* won the Academy Award for Best Original Screenplay.

The World Cup

In 2010, Spain's star-studded soccer team won the World Cup, soccer's world championship event. From David Villa to Iker Casillas to Andrés Iniesta (left), the Spanish team took to the field prepared to dominate and score. Under the guidance of coach Vicente del Bosque, the Red Fury stormed its way to victory by not conceding a single goal in the last four games of the tournament. When the clock ran out, all of Spain erupted with pride.

Sports

Soccer, called fútbol, is by far the most popular sport in Spain. La Liga is the national league in which the teams Real Madrid and FC Barcelona play. Games are shown on television and broadcast on radio. The stands are packed for every game, and

The stadium where Real Madrid plays holds more than eighty-five thousand fans.

the major soccer matches become the number one show of the week when they are broadcast. The top teams compete in the European Championship and the Confederations Cup.

Spain enjoys more than three hundred days of sunshine each year. Water sports—swimming, sailing, waterskiing, and speedboat racing—attract tourists to Spain's thousands of beaches. Tennis has become increasingly popular, as Rafael Nadal has become one of the world's top tennis players. Golf is another sport that has caught on in sunny Spain.

A sport called *pádel* (paddle tennis) is played throughout Spain and Latin America. It is played with wooden paddles on

Rafael Nadal is considered one of the greatest tennis players of all time. He is renowned for his speed and consistency.

Bullfighting: Right or Wrong?

Bullfighting is the traditional contest between a *matador* (bullfighter) and a *toro* (bull). It requires skill, daring, and knowledge of how to handle a bull that weighs up to 1,300 pounds (600 kilograms).

The spectacle begins with a procession, followed by the piercing of the bull's back by *banderilleros*, people who assist the matador, with barbed sticks. The idea is to weaken the bull before the matador enters the ring. At the end, the matador kills the bull.

Because of its cruelty to the animals, some regions in Spain have banned bullfighting in recent years. Since 2007, Spain has one-third fewer bullfights than it did in previous years. Catalonia, a former center of bullfighting, is one region that has banned the practice.

courts about half the size of a tennis court. In pádel, there are two players on each team. The ball is similar to a tennis ball and is served underhand. The court is surrounded by walls, and, like squash or racquetball, shots can be rebounded off the walls. The game is easy to learn and is popular at seaside resorts.

Bicycle and car racing both have large fan bases in Spain. Bicycle races can last for one day or many weeks. Alberto Contador won the 2008 Vuelta a España and the 2009 Tour de France. Fernando Alonso, a Formula 1 racer, is shaking up the standings as he dashes to win on courses all over the world. Car racing fans roar with approval as they watch the vehicles zoom around the track at 190 miles per hour (300 kph). Cycling and car racing are also shown on television and draw huge audiences whenever Spain's athletes are in the lead.

Food, Fun, and Family

EMILIA AND SERGIO ARE WORKING FURIOUSLY WITH their friends on building a *falla* for their neighborhood. A falla is a puppet or doll, but it is not just any puppet. The puppets are constructed of wood, cardboard, and papier-mâché—and are more than two stories high! Fallas represent a neighborhood and make fun of politicians and celebrities during Las Fallas, a five-day festival in Valencia honoring St. Joseph, the patron saint of carpenters. The festival features fireworks, feasting, and flames. At the end of the celebration, the fallas are lit on fire. Las Fallas is just one of the many colorful events that take place in Spain.

Opposite: **Giant puppets are burned at the Las Fallas festival. Lighting the fires is considered a way of welcoming spring.**

Celebrations

In Spain, families look forward to local holidays, called fiestas. These holidays may celebrate local harvests, an event from history, or a patron saint—a saint associated with a particular place. Most occur in the spring or summer, and can include activities such as dancing and concerts or bullfighting, parades, or fireworks.

A woman sells wooden roses on St. George's Day.

On St. George's Day, April 23, people in Catalonia give loved ones books and red roses. In July, bulls race through the streets during the Festival of San Fermín in Pamplona. One of the strangest celebrations is the festival of La Tomatina, held

The Running of the Bulls

Each year, men and women race through the streets of Pamplona being chased by bulls. This extremely dangerous tradition is part of the Festival of San Fermín. The runners get a head start, and then the bulls are released. The runners, who must be at least eighteen years old, lead the bulls into the bullring. Thousands of runners take part every year. Two or three hundred people are injured every year, mostly from tripping and not from being hurt by a bull.

in the town of Buñol in August. At this fiesta, people compete in a huge tomato fight.

National holidays are a mix of religious holidays and major national events. New Year's falls during the two-week Christmas season. New Year's Eve is a night for dinner with friends and family that lasts until very late. At midnight, as church bells chime or the seconds are counted down on television, party-goers eat one grape for each stroke of the clock. After eating twelve grapes, everyone wishes each other a happy new year. Christmas season ends with Three Kings Day on January 6.

An estimated 150,000 tomatoes are smashed during La Tomatina.

Carnaval is a fun celebration that occurs in February or early March. During Carnaval, there are parties, parades, costumes, and delicious food. Carnaval comes right before the solemn forty-day period called Lent. During Lent, people make sacrifices such as fasting, or not eating at certain times. Many people give up favorite foods. Lent leads up to Easter. The week before Easter is Semana Santa (Holy Week). Nobody goes to work or to school during that week.

Labor Day and National Day are nonreligious holidays. On Labor Day, May 1, groups hold parades to honor the military and

Workers parade through the streets on May 1, Labor Day.

National Holidays

New Year's Day	January 1
Three Kings Day	January 6
Holy Week	March or April
Easter	March or April
Easter Monday	March or April
Labor Day	May 1
National Day	October 12
All Saints' Day	November 1
Constitution Day	December 6
Immaculate Conception	December 8
Christmas Season	December 24–January 6

workers. There are picnics, feasts, and plenty of entertainment. National Day takes place on October 12, which is the date Christopher Columbus landed in the Americas. National Day honors the emergence of a worldwide Spanish presence.

The last nonreligious holiday of the year in Spain is Constitution Day on December 6. It commemorates the official signing of the constitution that brought democracy to Spain in 1978. As with other holidays, most government offices, businesses, and schools are closed on this day.

In the Home

Most Spanish families live in apartments, brick or stone buildings from three to five stories high. Families usually own the apartments they live in. The apartments are small with two or three bedrooms, a kitchen, a dining room, and a living room. Most family time is spent in the living room.

Tiny towns dot the Spanish countryside.

Some people own single-family homes. Many of these are in suburbs. Suburban housing is a mix of single-family homes and apartment buildings. Aragon, Castile, León, and the south tend to have small communities of houses where farmers live. The workers commute to their farmland. In other areas, farmers live in small houses on their farms. Farm families may consist of many generations of a family, including grandparents, aunts, uncles, and cousins, living together and working the land together.

Mealtime

In Spain, meals include breakfast, lunch, and dinner, and some significant snacks. Breakfast is a simple meal. Adults have coffee with milk, a sweet roll, or churros, which are like crullers. Children might have hot chocolate and churros. Cold cereal is also popular. *Torrija*, which is something like French toast, is a warm breakfast dish that is especially delicious topped with sugar and cinnamon.

Lunch is the big meal of the day. Eaten at 2:00 p.m., lunch may be several courses, including an appetizer, soup or salad, the main course, and dessert. Traditionally, Spaniards took a two-hour nap after lunch, so shops were closed from about 2:00 p.m. to 4:30 or 5:00 p.m. This tradition is no longer as common as it once was. People live too far from their work to go home for a nap, and businesses insist on a standard eight-hour workday. In most cities, lunch is now from 2:00 to about 3:30, followed by the finish of the workday.

Favorite Spanish Foods

chorizo	spicy pork sausage
churros	crispy fried dough to dip in chocolate
cordero asado	roast lamb
estofado de pollo	chicken stew
flan	baked vanilla custard
gambas al ajillo	shrimp with garlic
gazpacho	cold tomato soup
paella	rice and seafood dish

In Spain, the last meal is served late, sometimes at 11:00 p.m. It is a lighter meal, usually bread, cold meats, fruit, and cheese. Green salads or vegetables are also popular.

Heading home after a late-night meal out, many people stop for a cup of thick, creamy hot chocolate and more churros, which they dip in the chocolate. Delicious!

What's on the Menu?

Spain does not have one specific style of food, or cuisine. Each region has its own specialties and staple dishes. Regions along the coast serve more seafood than inland regions do. Pork is a

Churros with chocolate is a popular and delicious Spanish snack.

Gazpacho

This delicious cold soup is refreshing on a hot summer's day. Have an adult help you with this recipe.

Ingredients

6 ripe tomatoes

1 purple onion

2 cucumbers

1 red bell pepper

1 teaspoon garlic, minced

2 tablespoons fresh parsley, finely chopped

¼ cup olive oil

1 teaspoon salt

¼ cup red wine vinegar

2 tablespoons lemon juice

½ teaspoon black pepper

2 cups tomato juice

Directions

Peel the tomatoes, onion, and cucumbers. Remove the seeds of the cucumbers and bell pepper. Finely chop all the vegetables and put them in a large bowl. Add other ingredients and mix thoroughly. Refrigerate the soup for at least two to three hours before serving. Enjoy!

staple throughout most of Spain, and there are even regional flavors of ham and regional preferences for cooking it.

Andalusia, the southernmost region of Spain, is one of the world's major producers of olive oil. The region is coastal and warm, which makes for a long growing season. A classic Andalusian meal starts with gazpacho, which is followed by fried fish, or thinly sliced ham, and fresh fruit. Andalusia is the place to find Spain's finest hams—*Jabugo* and *bellota*.

Olive oil is one of Spain's most important products.

The coastal region of Valencia is known for its rice dishes, such as *paella valenciana*, a mixture of rice, fish, seafood, meat, saffron, vegetables, and onions. It is the combination of ingredients that makes paella so flavorful.

The people of Castile, in north-central Spain, tend to make a lot of dishes from foods grown in that region. The area is rich with wheat and barley, sheep and goats. Winter fare often consists of garbanzo beans, lentils, or dried beans in thick stews or soups. Shepherds in the hills make a quick meal of sliced bread fried with olive oil, ground pepper, and bacon. This dish, called *migas de pastor*, makes a quick breakfast or lunch for those tending their flocks. Because Castile is a region for raising sheep and pigs, the two traditional roast dinners are grilled lamb and roast suckling pig. Winter is also the time for butchering hogs and making chorizo, Spanish spiced sausage.

Paella has become popular around the world.

A grandfather pushes a baby carriage along the streets of Marbella in southern Spain. Spaniards live to be an average of eighty-one years old.

In the Basque region, people eat plenty of fish. Along the coast, fishers bring home weakfish, bonito, and tuna. Sardines and anchovies are processed in olive oil and served in salads and stews. Some of the most flavorful dishes are hake in green sauce and a stew of chopped bonito, potatoes, and olive oil.

What to Wear

Spaniards are quite particular about their clothing. Style and quality are important. Spain has its own fashion industry, and both men and women try to dress in the best styles. In business, men wear dark suits, shirts with collars, and ties. Women in business wear conservative dresses or slacks and leather shoes.

Young couples dress up to go out in the evening. Jeans and T-shirts are not viewed as acceptable to wear when going out to dinner or to the theater. Students in private schools wear uniforms.

The boys have sweaters or jackets and ties, and the girls wear skirts and blouses or jumpers, along with sweaters or jackets.

The Family

Family relationships are important in Spain. Though extended families don't live under the same roof as often as they used to, the family ties are still strong.

For centuries it was common for Spanish families to have six or eight children. Grandparents lived with their children and grandchildren in large, extended families. Today, Spanish families are much smaller than they used to be. The average woman has only one child. Children live with their parents while they are in school. Some may stay with their parents until they marry. Since Spaniards are getting married later—in their late twenties and early thirties—children may continue to live with their parents until they are thirty or older. The elderly, when they can no longer care for themselves, sometimes move into

Just for Fun

Young children play many different games during recess and after school. *Tiente* and *zapatito inglés* are Spanish versions of tag and red light, green light. A popular children's game is *cadeneta*, or little chain. One person is "it." Everyone runs around, and the person who is "it" tries to touch the others. Each touched person holds hands with the previously touched person, joining the chain. The game is over when everyone has been touched and a long chain is formed.

senior care facilities. For the wealthy, senior care may be quite elegant. For the poor, there are government-sponsored homes.

In cities, both parents usually work. This is a big change that has come about within the last forty years. In the past, the father was the head of the household, and the mother did the housework and raised the children. Today, housework and parenting are becoming shared responsibilities. Women are more likely to have college degrees now, so more jobs are available to them. It is only in recent years that women have held executive positions in large companies.

Marriage was once a strictly religious event. Now, though, civil weddings are more common. Spanish couples tend to have long engagements, primarily so they can save up for an

A father and son enjoy a trip to the park in Sevilla. Spanish fathers are more involved in child rearing than they once were.

Getting Married

In Spain, most brides carry orange blossoms. Before the ceremony, the groom traditionally gives the bride thirteen gold coins, which she carries in a small purse to her wedding. The coins represent the groom's promise to support his bride. For many years, Spanish brides wore black silk wedding dresses with black lace veils or shawls. Today, most Spanish brides wear white. Catholics still marry in the church, but many choose to get married in a nonreligious ceremony.

apartment and not have to live with either set of parents. Men get married at an average age of thirty-three and women at thirty-one. The bride and groom are likely to pay for their own wedding. A one-week honeymoon at a luxury resort is the ideal for most newlyweds. Instead of presents, most Spanish wedding guests give the couple cash so that they can pay for the wedding and honeymoon.

Ceremonies and traditions are also important at the end of life. When a loved one dies, a funeral ceremony is held the day after the death. Burial takes place within two days. In the Spanish tradition, family and close friends wear *luto*, which are black mourning clothes. In small towns and villages, widows and widowers may wear black mourning for the rest of their lives. On the anniversary of a loved one's death, family may gather for a Catholic service to honor the dead. In Spain, from birth to death, the most important life events draw family together.

Timeline

Spanish History		World History	
Homo antecessor lives in Spain and leaves behind bones and teeth.	**1.2 million years ago**		
Neanderthals live along the Iberian coast.	**150,000 years ago**		
Humans living in the Altamira cave paint the cave walls.	**37,000–12,000** BCE		
Stone Age hunter-gatherers live along the Mediterranean Sea.	**15,000-10,000** BCE	**ca. 2500** BCE	Egyptians build the pyramids and the Sphinx in Giza.
Phoenicians trade with Spaniards along the coast.	**1000** BCE	**ca. 563** BCE	The Buddha is born in India.
Roman troops invade Spain.	**218** BCE		
The Visigoths from Germany conquer Spain.	**573** CE	**313** CE	The Roman emperor Constantine legalizes Christianity.
Muslims from northern Africa gain control of Spain.	**711**	**610**	The Prophet Muhammad begins preaching a new religion called Islam.
		1054	The Eastern (Orthodox) and Western (Roman Catholic) Churches break apart.
		1095	The Crusades begin.
Moorish control is reduced to the kingdom of Granada.	**1200**	**1215**	King John seals the Magna Carta.
		1300s	The Renaissance begins in Italy.
		1347	The plague sweeps through Europe.
		1453	Ottoman Turks capture Constantinople, conquering the Byzantine Empire.
Ferdinand marries Isabella, uniting Aragon and Castile.	**1469**		
Jews are forced out of Spain; Christopher Columbus sails to the Americas.	**1492**	**1492**	Columbus arrives in North America.
Vasco Núñez de Balboa, working for the Spanish crown, crosses Central America.	**1513**	**1500s**	Reformers break away from the Catholic Church, and Protestantism is born.

Spanish History

Hernán Cortés conquers the Aztecs.	1519
Francisco Pizarro conquers the Incas.	1533
The British navy defeats the Spanish Armada.	1588
Britain and Austria invade Spain during the War of Spanish Succession.	1701
The French army occupies Spain.	1808–1814
Spain loses the Spanish-American War.	1898
General Miguel Primo de Rivera becomes prime minister.	1923
The Second Spanish Republic is established.	1931
The Spanish Civil War begins.	1936
National rebels win the civil war; Francisco Franco becomes dictator.	1939
Francisco Franco dies.	1975
Spain joins the European Union.	1986
Spain hosts the Olympic Summer Games in Barcelona.	1992
Spain begins using the euro.	2002
Trains are bombed in Madrid, killing 191 people.	2004
Unemployment reaches 20 percent.	2008
Conservative leader Mariano Rajoy becomes prime minister.	2011

World History

1776	The U.S. Declaration of Independence is signed.
1789	The French Revolution begins.
1865	The American Civil War ends.
1879	The first practical lightbulb is invented.
1914	World War I begins.
1917	The Bolshevik Revolution brings communism to Russia.
1929	A worldwide economic depression begins.
1939	World War II begins.
1945	World War II ends.
1957	The Vietnam War begins.
1969	Humans land on the Moon.
1975	The Vietnam War ends.
1989	The Berlin Wall is torn down as communism crumbles in Eastern Europe.
1991	The Soviet Union breaks into separate states.
2001	Terrorists attack the World Trade Center in New York City and the Pentagon near Washington, D.C.
2004	A tsunami in the Indian Ocean destroys coastlines in Africa, India, and Southeast Asia.
2008	The United States elects its first African American president.

Fast Facts

Official name: Kingdom of Spain

Capital: Madrid

Official languages: Castilian Spanish, Aranese, Catalan, Euskara, and Galician

Madrid

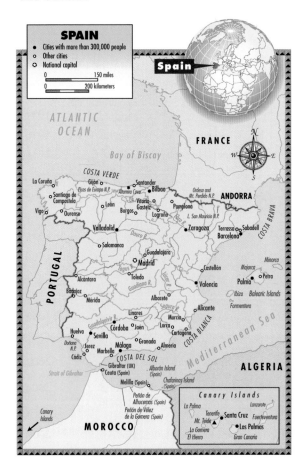

Spanish flag

Official religion:	None
National anthem:	"La marcha real" ("The Royal March")
Government:	Parliamentary monarchy
Chief of state:	Monarch
Head of government:	Prime minister
Constitution:	Adopted 1978
Bordering countries:	Portugal, France, Andorra
Area:	194,897 square miles (504,781 sq km)
Highest elevation:	Mount Teide on Tenerife in the Canary Islands, 12,198 feet (3,718 m) above sea level
Lowest elevation:	Atlantic Ocean, at sea level
Longest river:	Ebro, 565 miles (910 km)
Largest lake:	Sanabria, 909 acres (368 hectares)
Length of coastline:	3,084 miles (4,963 km)
Average low temperature:	In Madrid, 32°F (0°C) in January; 61°F (16°C) in July
Average high temperature:	In Madrid, 52°F (11°C) in January; 90°F (32°C) in July
Average annual precipitation:	In Madrid, 17 inches (43 cm)
National population (2011 est.):	46,754,784

Cascada del Cinca

Cathedral of Santiago
de Compostela

Population of major cities (2010 est.):	Madrid	3,273,049
	Barcelona	1,673,075
	Valencia	809,267
	Sevilla	705,107
	Zaragoza	701,090

Landmarks:
▶ *Alhambra,* Granada

▶ *Aqueduct,* Segovia

▶ *Cathedral of Santiago de Compostela,* Santiago de Compostela

▶ *Cave of Altamira,* Altamira

▶ *Doñana National Park,* Andalusia

▶ *Prado Museum,* Madrid

Economy: The service industry is at the heart of the Spanish economy. Tourism is particularly important, with Spain being the fifth most visited country in the world. Important industries in Spain include iron and steel production, electronics, textiles and apparel, and food and beverages. Coal, copper, lead, and iron are mined in Spain. Important agricultural products include olives, oranges, wheat, wine grapes, sugar beets, pork, beef, poultry, and dairy products.

Currency: The euro. In 2012, 0.76 euros equaled 1 U.S. dollar.

System of weights and measures: Metric system

Literacy rate: 98%

Currency

Schoolchildren

Pablo Picasso

Common Spanish words and phrases:

buenos días	good morning
buenas tardes	good afternoon
adiós	good-bye
¿Cómo está usted?	How are you?
Muy bien.	I'm fine.
sí	yes
no	no
perdón	excuse me
gracias	thank you
de nada	you're welcome
¿Puede usted ayudarme?	Can you help me?

Prominent Spaniards:

Pedro Almodóvar (1949–)
Filmmaker

Miguel de Cervantes (1547–1616)
Writer

Hernán Cortés (1485–1547)
Conqueror of the Aztec Empire

Penélope Cruz (1974–)
Actress

Francisco Franco (1892–1975)
Dictator

Moses Maimonides (1135–1204)
Philosopher and physician

Pablo Picasso (1881–1973)
Painter

Diego Velázquez (1599–1660)
Painter

To Find Out More

Books

- ▶ Ancona, George. *¡Olé! Flamenco.* New York: Lee & Low, 2010.

- ▶ Croy, Anita. *Spain.* Washington, DC: National Geographic, 2010.

- ▶ Feinstein, Stephen. *Columbus: Opening Up the New World.* Berkeley Heights, NJ: Enslow Publishers, 2009.

- ▶ Serres, Alain. *And Picasso Painted Guernica.* Sydney, Australia: Allen & Unwin, 2010.

Music

- ▶ Bisbal, David. *Sin mirar atras. (Without Looking Back).* Universal Latino, 2009.

- ▶ La Oreja de Van Gogh. *Cometas por el cielo (Comets in the Sky).* Sony, 2011.

- ▶ Sanz, Alejandro. *No es lo mismo (It Is Not the Same).* Warner Music Latina, 2003.

▶ Visit this Scholastic Web site for more information on Spain:
www.factsfornow.scholastic.com
Enter the keyword **Spain**

Index

Page numbers in *italics* indicate illustrations.

Meet the Author

BARBARA SOMERVILL BEGAN LEARNING ABOUT SPAIN when she was in elementary school. Years of study and an appreciation for the culture of Spain helped her find material for this book. Somervill has been writing children's nonfiction books for more than a dozen years. She learns something new every day as she does her research. Many years ago, her Spanish professor from Andalusia gave her the recipe for gazpacho that is in this book. It is a family favorite, and she hopes you enjoy it.

Photo Credits